ICE AND SNOW NEAR THE GANGES' SOURCE

NALTA, A GLACIAL LAKE IN THE KARAKORAMS

LIFE NATURE LIBRARY
LIFE SCIENCE LIBRARY
GREAT AGES OF MAN
FOODS OF THE WORLD
TIME-LIFE LIBRARY OF ART
LIFE LIBRARY OF PHOTOGRAPHY
THE EMERGENCE OF MAN
THE OLD WEST
THE ART OF SEWING
THE GREAT CITIES

THE HIMALAYAS

THE WORLD'S WILD PLACES/TIME-LIFE BOOKS/AMSTERDAM

BY NIGEL NICOLSON
AND THE EDITORS OF TIME-LIFE BOOKS

THE WORLD'S WILD PLACES

Editorial Staff for *The Himalayas*:
EDITOR: John Man
Deputy Editor: Christopher Farman
Picture Editor: Pamela Marke
Design Consultant: Louis Klein
Staff Writers:
Michael Brown, Mally Cox, Kate Dorment,
Dan Freeman, Heather Sherlock,
Timberlake Wertenbaker
Art Director: Graham Davis
Assistant Art Director: Roy Williams
Design Assistant: Joyce Mason
Picture Researchers:
Karin Pearce, Susan Stratton
Editorial Researcher: Vanessa Kramer
Editorial Co-ordinator: Jackie Matthews

Consultants
Botany: Christopher Grey-Wilson, Phyllis Edwards
Invertebrates: Michael Tweedie
Geology: Dr. Peter Stubbs
Geomorphology: John Tyson
Ornithology: I. J. Ferguson-Lees
Zoology: Dr. P. J. K. Burton

The captions and text of the picture essays are written
by the staff of Time-Life Books.

Valuable assistance was given in the preparation of
this volume by the following Time-Life correspondents:
Elizabeth Hawley, Kathmandu, and Jim Shepherd,
New Delhi.

Published by Time-Life International (Nederland) B.V.
5 Ottho Heldringstraat, Amsterdam 18

The Author: Nigel Nicolson first visited Nepal for two weeks in 1965, and has subsequently spent almost four months in the Himalayas in order to write this book. An accomplished author of many books on architecture, history, and politics, his most recent ones include *Portrait of a Marriage*, and *Alex*, a widely acclaimed biography of Field Marshal Earl Alexander of Tunis.

The Consultant: Lord Hunt of Llanvair Waterdine is a distinguished mountaineer who led the successful assault on Mount Everest in 1953. Other expeditions have taken him to Russia, Greenland, Greece and Poland. He is a strong supporter of international mountaineering projects. Among the books he has written are: *The Ascent of Everest* and *The Red Snows*.

The Cover: Beyond a shadow-darkened ridge in north-west Jammu-Kashmir, Nanga Parbat soars 26,660 feet into the clouds. Thirty men died climbing this peak before it was conquered by a German and Austrian team in 1953.

Contents

The World's Highest Mountain Chain

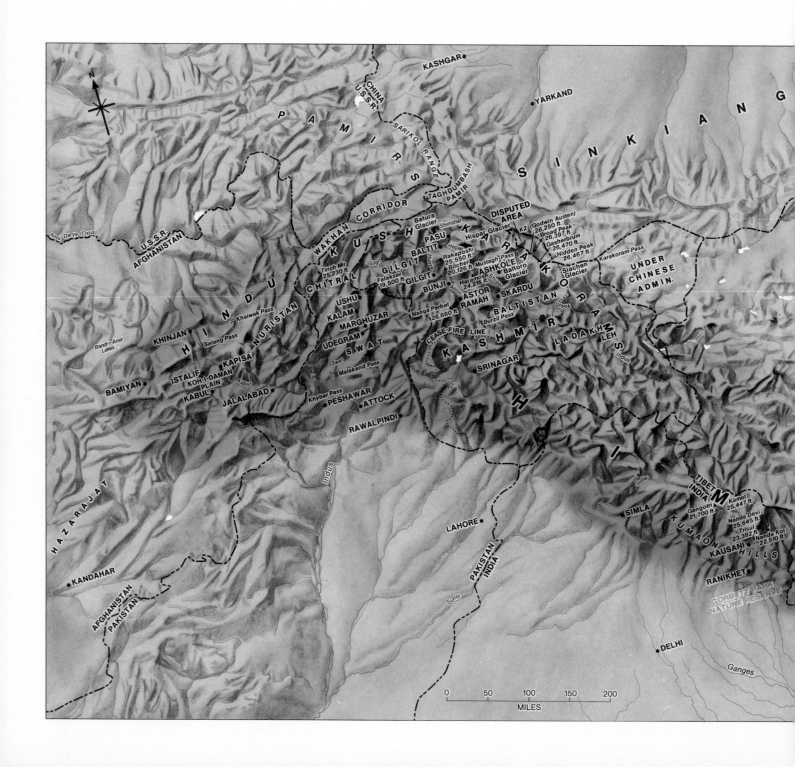

The extensive mountain chain, the Himalayas, indicated by the green rectangle on the outline map (right), stretches across the thick neck of the Indian sub-continent for about 1,700 miles, from Afghanistan in the west to Assam in the south-east. Roughly 100 to 150 miles wide, it straddles six countries, dividing India from Tibet. Distinguished by enormous variety of climate, vegetation and wild life, the mountain chain consists of three major ranges: the Himalayas, the Karakorams and the Hindu Kush. Lush tropical valleys and snow-capped peaks dominate the Himalayas and Karakorams, while the Hindu Kush in the far west lies beyond the reach of the monsoons and therefore has much bleaker slopes. On the relief map (below) dark green stands for vegetation up to the treeline at 12,000 feet; light green represents the alpine zone at 15,000 feet. Nature reserves and national parks are in red. Passes are marked) (. Peaks are indicated by a triangle. Rivers and lakes are in blue.

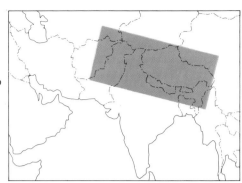

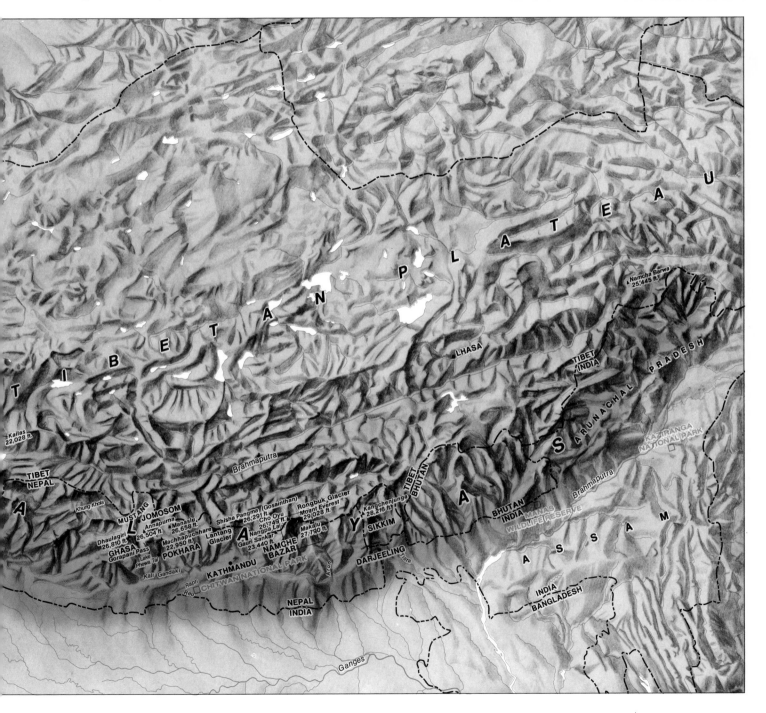

1/ Abode of Snow

---

*A hundred divine epochs would not suffice to describe
all the marvels of the Himalayas.*   SANSKRIT PROVERB

Some years ago I flew from Delhi to Moscow. The clouds rolled in heavily
over Delhi's airport, and with the resigned despondency of all long-
distance travellers I foresaw a dull, tiring flight. But gloom and clouds
can both be penetrated. The clouds persisted until Moscow, but within a
few minutes from take-off we rose above them. I glanced out of the
window. There, piercing the clouds, was a sight that made me grip my
neighbour's arm. "Look!" I cried, "the Himalayas!" He was not
impressed: I had spilled his coffee.

I had never seen them before, and there they were, or at least the
middle section of them, from Kashmir to Nepal, stretched across the
wide angle of my vision at a mean distance of 200 miles. My first impression was of their whiteness; the second of their regularity; the third of
their unexpected smallness. The range rose suddenly as a toothed ridge
above the plain of the clouds, taut as the blade of a band-saw, glitter-
white in the sun, its narrowness accentuated by its length. It seemed to
me a small protuberance for so great an earth. But five vertical miles
were dwarfed by the 500 horizontal miles I could see from the aeroplane.

Something of their immensity became clearer as we flew close to the
Karakorams, the north-west section of the Himalayas in northern
Kashmir. The range now appeared like a coastline, the clouds a grey sea
washing its feet and penetrating its fjords. The ground was heavily
broken, and black began to appear against the white, the black of huge

rock faces too steep to hold the snow. I was able to distinguish individual peaks: K2, the second highest in the world; Nanga Parbat, which killed 30 men before it was climbed. Their beauty was cruel, terrifyingly silent. They assumed defiant attitudes, basically pyramidal in deference to the only law that they were forced to acknowledge, the law of gravity, but their crowns were formed by geological accident—sharp as thorns, or domed and sullen. They seemed to possess every characteristic of living people.

Nine years later I returned to the Himalayas for this book with photographer Terry Spencer. Now we confronted them without the advantage of a height greater than their own. At dusk I looked out from the Indian village that was our base, towards the huge mountain-island of Nanda Devi and Nanda Kot 30 miles away, an island because both peaks are separated from their neighbours by vast ravines on each side. Nanda Devi, 25,645 feet high, is considered by many the pearl of the Himalayas, so symmetrical, so simple that a child could draw it, the double peaks linked by a straight edge as fine as a chisel's, the blade formed by a 10,000-foot ice-wall, grooved but immaculate.

Our village was called Kausani, which crowns a high ridge where Mahatma Gandhi once spent three months writing one of his best-known books, *Anashakti Yog.* The man in charge of his bungalow, now a shrine, said that we could stay there the night if we wished, but there were certain rules. We asked what they were. "First you must take off your shoes." We took off our shoes. "You must not eat meat while you are in this place." I wondered, but did not dare ask, whether eggs counted as meat, for hard-boiled eggs were all we had brought with us. "Next," he said, "we have a service in memory of the Mahatma every evening at six sharp." There is no person in the recent history of the East whose memory I revere more greatly, but we both knew instinctively that neither in body nor in spirit were we worthy to occupy Gandhi's bungalow even for a single night. We managed to find rooms in a government rest-house a little way along the ridge. It was very uncomfortable, but we had a magnificent view of Nanda Devi.

Below us the ground fell away in terraces to a deep valley and then mounted again to another ridge, and beyond it to another, and then another, respectively the gallery, dress-circle and stalls facing a vast proscenium. We saw before us a frontier written against the sky, an ultimate lift of the earth's surface, a frontier between much more than India and Tibet, for it divides climates, cultures, religions and centuries. It is the most authentic wilderness in the world. Men can inhabit swamps and deserts and even polar wastes, but few living things can exist for long in the frozen fastness that we saw so clearly from so safe a distance. Ruled out of bounds by their permanent covering of snow, the upper few thousand feet were spectacular seen through binoculars. Himalaya means "Abode of Snow". There lay its roof-top. The ridges rode upwards supported by precipices to such needle-points that if it were architecture one could not believe that stone thus suspended could retain its stability.

Occasionally a small cloud hitched itself to a peak and flew for an hour like a tattered pennant, but most of the range remained untarnished-white until shortly before sundown. The light then dropped like sound receding. The valleys, last to receive it, first to lose it, returned to the lap of darkness, but for long afterwards the snow-mountains were swept by colour. Nothing changes in mountains but visibility and the intensity of light, Promethean light upon Promethean rock, one elemental force reacting upon another.

The clouds, streakily horizontal or rising in flares, now gathered huger than the mountains but made them seem higher, just as a man swaddled in bedclothes seems taller than when upright. As the sun sank, the clouds retained its light till at last they were little balls of filmy gauze, such as you see accompanied by cherubim in the background of Italian paintings. Then rose the full moon, the great compensator, and late that night I left my bed to discover whether it could restore the mountains to me. It did, vestigially. If I had not known that they were there, I would have doubted what I saw: sheets of distant whiteness, rhomboid-shaped, like yachts in mist, pale, irregular and spectral.

A third scene comes to my mind, no longer from outside the Himalayas but from within them. We were camped on the western slopes of Annapurna. It had been a hard day's walking, and fearing to risk the precipitous path in darkness, Terry and I decided to call a halt. We pitched our tents in a small field on the valley floor, and sat over the camp-fire between them. Suddenly I spotted a brilliant point of light almost directly overhead.

"It's a planet," I said.

"No planet is as bright as that," said Terry.

"Then it's Skylab."

"No, it's not moving."

"I know," I said, with sudden inspiration. "It's the Kohoutek comet," of which the imminent approach had just been announced.

"Far too soon for that," Terry replied.

Then what? We consulted our head porter, a Sherpa. He laughed. "It's a shepherd's bonfire." It did not seem possible. The thing was in the sky. But he was right, as we saw clearly when daylight returned. Darkness had not only obliterated detail; it had erased from our short-lived memories the gradient of the mountainside. From its five linked peaks, Annapurna does not flow or tumble to man-level. It shoots down. We had been looking at a spot barely 2,000 feet over our heads. The mountain rose a further 20,000 feet above it.

In all our travels I never experienced a more dramatic reminder of the scale of the Himalayas. It is well known that they contain the greatest mountains on earth, but few people realize how much greater they are than any others. In all of North America the highest peak is 20,320 feet (Mount McKinley, Alaska); in the Andes, Aconcagua (22,834); in Africa, Kilimanjaro (19,340); in Europe, Mont Blanc (15,781); in Australasia, Mount Cook (12,349). But in the Himalayas, Karakorams and Hindu Kush, all connected geologically and ecologically, there are three peaks —Everest, K2 and Kangchenjunga—over 28,000 feet, and 13 others over 26,000. Their names are as majestic as their appearance: Lhotse, Makalu, Dhaulagiri, Cho Oyu, Nanga Parbat, Manaslu, Annapurna I and II, Hidden Peak, Broad Peak, Gasherbrum II, Shisha Pangma (also named Gosainthan), Gasherbrum IV. So many others exceed in height the tallest mountains elsewhere in the world that while they have now all been mapped, comparatively few have been named.

The Himalayas, Karakorams and Hindu Kush cover by their joint length of some 1,700 miles parts of six countries: India (including Sikkim), Bhutan, Nepal, Pakistan, China (including Tibet) and Afghanistan. The Pamirs are also geographically part of the group, but spring away from it northwards, and are outside the scope of this book.

The Himalayas do not make a neat pattern on a relief map. They present no clean arc like the Alps, no line as firmly ruled as the Andes. The range runs north-east through Afghanistan, east and south through Kashmir, south-east through India, east through Nepal, Sikkim and Bhutan, and north-east again to the Brahmaputra. The foothills on the "Indian" side would qualify on most maps as considerable mountain ranges by themselves, while the high plateau of Tibet and its continuation into southern China maintain a general level of 15,000 feet, splashing the map with wide areas of a disconcerting dark brown and speckling it with the white of permanent snow. One would be tempted to ask: Where are the Himalayas?

On the ground it is different. Nobody standing on a hilltop in the Kumaons or on the airfield of Pokhara in central Nepal would have any doubt where the Himalayas are. At Pokhara the valley floor lies at 2,900 feet. In front, with scarcely an intervening foothill, rises Machhapuchhare, nearly 23,000 feet high, and beyond it, the colossal curve of the Annapurnas, five summits in a row. In no place on earth is there so great a vertical rise in so short a horizontal distance.

The Himalayas demand superlatives. They *are* superlative: the highest mountain, the highest pass, the deepest gorge, the highest-living animals—the mountains confront us with phenomena that exist nowhere else on earth. Other mountain ranges can be digested by the landscape: they are penetrable, harnessed by roads and railways. But no railways cross the Himalayas, and few roads. They are mountains so stupendous that they can be overflown, but not tunnelled; climbed, but never tamed; mapped, but seldom visited. They are, and look like, what Kenneth Mason, formerly a Superintendent of the Survey of India, has called "the greatest physical feature of the earth". Why do they reach so high? Why, to twist the famous phrase, *why* are they there?

In Kathmandu I met a young French geologist. I do not like geology because I do not understand its language, but I very much liked this geologist, because he was able to explain to me by two simple gestures how the Himalayas were formed.

First he held his hands palms down, fingers pointing inwards, some six inches apart, and slowly moved one hand into the other. His fingers bent under pressure; some folded downwards to lie alongside each other, but most yielded upwards into peaks.

"My hands," he said, "are two continents. When they meet, and if pressure is maintained, two things can happen. They can fold under each other; or they can be forced into the air. The Himalayas are my upper fingers, the buckled edges of two continents that clashed."

"But if they were forced up as you say, why are they so pointed? After all, rocks aren't like your fingers. They lose their shape under pressure. One would have expected a tumbled mass, not those elegant pyramids and spires."

Then he gave me his second demonstration. He held up one hand, vertically, and separated his fingers. The gaps between them represented the valleys and glaciers—the fissures—and he explained that rocks can be easily cut by water, ice, wind, landslide and avalanche into sharp shapes. He pointed to his middle finger: "Machhapuchhare!" he said with a smile, and strode off.

A shaggy male yak pauses briefly from his grazing on grass and lichen in one of the few photographs ever taken of the wild yak in its natural environment. Hunted almost to extinction, most of the wild yak have retreated to the remotest heights of the 15,000-foot Tibetan plateau. During spring the yak's under-fur—which in winter insulates it from temperatures of −40° F.— moults, giving it this dishevelled look.

I had never wondered before why mountains exist. To me they had simply been part of the natural scene. But mountains are not that permanent. Enormous pressures built them, pressures exerted by the movement of primeval continents, in a continuing process known to geologists as Continental Drift. Continents, or pieces of the continents as we know them, and all the oceans, are carried on rafts or "plates" some 40 miles thick, and these plates float on the viscous rock beneath the earth's crust. They move with inexorable slowness, from half an inch to four inches in a year, away from or towards each other. When they move away, new ocean floors form in their wake; when they collide, they raise mountains because their coastal and submarine rocks, after a bit of undershuffling, have no place to go but upwards.

This process, of course, is very gradual and began between 40 and 60 million years ago, when the plate bearing what was then the separate continent of India collided with that of the huge northern continent of Asia. But quite recently there came a climax. Between half a million and two million years ago the Himalayas shot up another 10,000 feet, at a rate unknown in any other geological event. They are, therefore, the youngest as well as the highest mountains in the world, and they are high because they are young. There has been no time for erosion to wear them down.

As you walk in the Himalayas, and if you have been taught to look for it, you can find evidence of these cataclysmic events. The first is the presence of fossilized sea-animals high up on the slopes. One day in central Nepal a boy brought me a round piece of dark-blue shale that he cracked open on a rock. Inside was the perfectly preserved fossil of an ammonite, a sea creature that flourished for hundreds of millions of years and then become extinct. These ammonites have been found in the Himalayas as high as 18,000 feet. The uppermost levels are limestone, a rock formed by the gradual deposit on the seabed of the shells of marine creatures. There can be only one explanation: as the continents collided and reared upwards at their edges, part of the original seabed between them was carried up with the deeper rocks.

Another and even more startling effect of Continental Drift is the direction taken by Himalayan rivers. One might have supposed that the greatest mountain range on earth would also form its most impressive watershed. The rain and melting snow must surely flow down the northern slopes into Tibet and down the southern slopes into the Indian plain. Instead they form rivers that cut through the relatively new and soft structure of the mountains on their way to the lowlands and the sea. In this respect, too, they are unique among the mountains of the

Under clumps of bankside grass, a swift glacial stream flows through a sharply-angled channel in rock 20,000 feet up on Annapurna South. The stripes are the tilted strata of alternating sediments— such as limestone and shale—that have been exposed by the water's persistent erosive action over thousands of years.

world. Thus, the great water-divide is not the crest-line of the mountains, but the edge of the Tibetan plateau, 100 miles to the north of it and, on average, 10,000 feet lower down.

The result is seen in the huge trans-Himalayan gorges, the deepest in the world. Two of the main rivers, the Indus and the Brahmaputra, which rise a few miles from each other in Tibet, wend nearly 1,000 miles west and east before they turn abruptly southwards to cut through the Himalayas to the Indian Ocean. But a smaller river like the Arun, which flows between the Everest massif and Kangchenjunga, rises 80 miles north of Everest and breaks directly through the chain in a gorge over 18,000 feet deep. (Its headwaters are less than two miles from the course of the Brahmaputra. The Arun, with its violently erosive strength and steep gradient, must sooner or later claw its way through this narrow watershed and "capture" the Brahmaputra, thus reducing one of the greatest rivers of the world to a miserable trickle.)

The geologists explain this curious phenomenon by supposing that the rivers must already have been there before the Himalayas rose to their present height. The Arun, and many others like it, found their natural way to the ocean southwards from the highest mountains then existing. When, in their final convulsion, the Himalayas topped the Tibetan mountains, the rivers were strong enough to hold their course through the rising barrier, cutting their gorges in the soft sedimentary rocks and the tougher granites.

The process is still not complete. The rocks are being forced upwards by the continuing pressure beneath them. It is difficult to gauge the rate of rise because measurements do not extend back for more than a century, but there is no doubt that the highest Himalayas are growing higher under the pressure of the still-merging continents. The annual growth has been calculated at between three and four inches. But this does not allow for erosion, and the net growth is estimated at a few inches a century. However, this is definite enough for a geologist to have warned mountaineers facetiously in 1952 that they must climb Everest before it became too high to climb. The British expedition did so in the following year.

Appalling disasters accompany the movement of the rocks. The huge natural forces of uplift and gravity and cleavage by ice and water can render futile man's attempts to control them. The Himalayas are a region of constant earthquake, landslip and flood. In 1841 a mass of rock from the west side of Nanga Parbat was precipitated into the Indus, holding back the waters to form a lake 40 miles long, and when a few months later the dam burst, the flood was catastrophic, drowning an entire Sikh army camped at Attock 100 miles lower down. The Nepal earthquake of 1934 killed more than 10,000 people.

Everywhere in the Himalayas one can see evidence of changes on a lesser scale. Turning the corner of a mountain path, I came upon a scene of devastation caused by a landslip only three weeks before. A fraction of a mountain spur, giving way suddenly in the middle of the night, had obliterated in a few seconds a fraction of human endeavour. It had sheared a path clean through a village centre. Twelve sleeping people were killed instantly. The timbers of their houses were strewn like matchsticks, and boulders as big as cottages lay heavily where cottages had stood. Five hundred feet above, the cliff showed a clean scar; five hundred feet below, the torrent of rocks lay expended on the valley floor. Such disasters will occur over and over again, unpredictably, when a last drop of surface-water tips the precarious balance. "Abode of Snow"! How homely a name for something so implacably cruel!

Yet these inhospitable carcasses of shifting rock are also sources of sustenance, and are feared and worshipped by their inhabitants. Annapurna means "Giver of Life" and the Tibetan name for the Everest group is Chomolungma, "Goddess Mother of the Earth." Their snows feed the valleys, water the animals and crops, nourish the primula and the pine. On their lower slopes the monsoon adds its heavy load to this massive process of irrigation.

The monsoon is not itself a rain, but a wind that carries rain. It originates in the Indian Ocean and, flowing water-laden across India, rides up the slopes of the mountains, expanding and cooling as it ascends. Eventually, the vapour condenses and rain pours down in torrents between April and mid-October, according to the longitude. "Upon what a gigantic scale does nature here operate!" wrote the British naturalist, Joseph Dalton Hooker, in 1848. "Vapours raised from an ocean whose nearest route is more than 400 miles distant are safely transported without the loss of one drop of water to support the rank luxuriance of this far distant region. This and other offices fulfilled, the waste waters are returned by the rivers to the ocean, and again exhaled, exported, recollected and returned!"

Today we express our admiration of nature less extravagantly, and also more precisely, because Hooker was wrong in attributing to the monsoon such miraculous powers of containment: on its way to the Himalayas it leaks considerably. On arrival it releases its water on the southern and middle slopes of the mountains. Above 20,000 feet little remains to fall, which is one reason why Everest's summit is usually seen as a pyramid of black rock; and none of it on the Tibetan plateau beyond. The Himalayas are a climatic barrier: southwards, they absorb the monsoon like a hydraulic buffer; northwards, they shield the plains from the cruel climate of Tibet, its searing summer winds and bitter winter gales. As it moves westwards, the monsoon's load decreases. At Darjeeling, on the border of Sikkim, the rainfall is 123 inches in the year; at Simla, north of Delhi, it is 63 inches; at Leh, in Kashmir, only three.

At the end of the rains, the climate of the monsoon Himalayas is delightful. In three months of travel I experienced only one short spatter of rain, and walked shirt-sleeved as high as 13,000 feet in sunshine that was unbroken for days on end, and in air so pure that a mountain peak 20 miles away appeared but five. In the mountains the temperature varies greatly from place to place and from hour to hour, so thin is the air and so intense the radiation. In the daytime you can suffer from sunstroke; at night from acute frostbite. When the temperature drops sharply at dusk, there is always (for the casual walker) the refuge of the plains, where true winter never comes. One is reluctant to seek it. The height lost must be painfully regained next day; and what is a horizon closed by nearby trees compared to the view at dawn from the upper hills, of sunlit mountains rising above gulfs of encircling mist?

The monsoon is partly responsible for the variety of Himalayan vegetation, but more important is the rapid change of altitude. Just as the southern slopes of the mountains are quite different from the northern, the first freshened by the monsoon and vigorous, the others bleak and sterile, so in ascending from the *terai*, or jungle, in the lower valleys to the tree-line and then the snow-line, one passes through botanical layers that could only be discovered in the flat lands of Europe and America by a south-north journey of 3,000 miles. If in the plains the temperature is 80°F., it will be −40°F. at the summit of Everest. Almost the whole range of the world's climate, and hence its flora and fauna, are concentrated within four or five vertical miles, from tropical jungle to frozen slopes.

The part of the *terai* that I visited was not particularly dense. The sal tree, which is its main constituent, is a fine, straight-limbed evergreen that discourages the undergrowth, and the jungle is more like a thick Western forest than the nightmare litter of decaying branches, weeds, vines and brambles, that I had imagined. The ground is clear, patinated by starry flowers. Much of the *terai* is open country, but only in the sense

One of the most eminent of 19th-Century scientists and a close confidant of Darwin, Sir Joseph Dalton Hooker (above) travelled through India to study the distribution and evolution of plant species. In 1848-50, he explored Sikkim where he discovered some 22 new species of rhododendron, a common Himalayan flowering shrub. Among these was the Rhododendron dalhousiae (shown right in Hooker's own drawing), named after Lady Dalhousie, wife of the then Governor-General of India.

of being treeless, for the view across it is even more restricted than in the jungle proper—by grasses and bamboo that by the autumn have grown as much as 25 feet high.

From the *terai* we worked our way up to Ranikhet in the Kumaon Hills, a vertical distance of some 8,000 feet, and by degrees, with deep interpenetration, the vegetation changed. The lower forest is alive with insect and animal life, rank with growth; the upper is distinguished by its silence. The sal gives place to pine, the pine to oak, the oak to juniper and rhododendron, and above that comes birch, which marks the tree-line. At intervals we found solitary specimens of maple, Indian horse-chestnut (*Aesculus india*), the silk-cotton tree, and the imported eucalyptus. The most interesting sight was a marvellous example of the banyan tree, trailing aerial roots until they anchored in the earth and grew as satellite trunks, turning a tree into a marquee.

Freaks like the banyan do not form forests. Of those trees that do, by far the loveliest are not the oaks, which in Asia have lost the graceful boles and crowns of their European and North American cousins, but the conifers. Here there are not only pines, but also spruce, larch, fir and juniper. They are old in geological time. They have stood in the snow and cold and darkness, yet are evergreen, reminders that all winters come to an end, that life endures. The king of them all in the Kumaons is the chir pine. They stride along a sky-silhouetted ridge, or in glades that sweep down slopes so steep that the roots of one are level with its neighbour's spire. The forest floor is thick with their fallen needles. These prevent intrusive growth, so that the view between their well-spaced trunks is unimpeded, and they wend to the valley bottoms like colonnades. Sometimes the chir will vary its slim triangular shape to grow tufts at intervals up the trunk, terminating in a spidery puff-ball at the top, a growth as unattractive as the tufts of hair on a clipped poodle and an indication that branches have been lopped off. It can, however, stand its endless symmetrical repetition, adorning rather than clothing the brown hills, and filling the air with the sweet scent of resin.

Where the trees have light and soil enough beneath them, or on the naked hillsides and above the line where the trees end, flowers grow in such profusion and variety that for many people the Himalayan region means primarily the greatest horticultural treasure-house on earth. I was not there at the season of their greatest blossoming, for like their dreaded companions, the leeches, they flourish best during the monsoon. But there is no need to visit the Himalayas in spring or summer to know their flowers: we can find them in our own gardens, thanks to the work of botanists like Joseph Dalton Hooker, Brian Hodgson, Bishop Heber, Frank Kingdon Ward and Frank Ludlow.

In the Himalayas, most of these flowers extend wild in sheets where the Western city-dweller would boast of a small patch. But some, like the Himalayan blue poppy, which the gardener would propagate to fill a bed, are often extremely elusive in their natural state. One of the joys of Himalayan travel is to find flowers in their greatest variety and numbers above 12,000 feet, between tree and snow, the scale of the flowers diminishing in inverse proportion to the enlargement of the landscape, and their colours deepening in the intensified ultra-violet rays of the sun. The primulas, purple-pink, blue, white and yellow, push up in early spring at the base of great cliffs or in sunny places under the shelter of giant boulders. Others emerge through the snow before it is melted, their buds and leaves wrapped in a scaly protective covering. In July, the meadows between 13,000 and 15,000 feet are bright with potentillas in their millions, anemones, *Corydalis*, several species of aconite and edelweiss, saxifrages, irises, asters, blue, lilac and white gentians (which carpet the ground), and the cotoneaster.

But the pride of the Himalayan flowers, particularly in the east, are the rhododendrons. Among the first shrubs to blossom, from February to April, before the monsoon has time to ravish them, they range from the tiny dwarf carpeter to the tall tree rhododendron, the national flower of Nepal. Flourishing as complete forests at heights between 5,000 and 10,000 feet, the blooms are a multitude of colours from scarlet to pure white. As a shrub, the rhododendron is easily transplantable, and has spread throughout the world. But how different are the clumps in the wilderness sections of large Edwardian gardens from the Himalayan species from which they emerged! In Nepal the tree rhododendrons grow as high as 60 feet, their dark brown limbs twisting like vegetable Laocoons, and staining red whole mountain-sides with their vivid and glorious abundance.

The flowers and the mountains—together they suggest the opposite ends of the scale on which nature works. At one extreme operate the vast, apocalyptic forces that created the mountains; at the other, the intricate subtleties that produced a perfect flower; the first beyond man's capacity to control; the second beyond his present capacity to comprehend. But both equally deserving of his awe.

The Shaping Ice

Since the onset of the first Ice Age nearly two million years ago, ice has been incessantly reshaping the Himalayas. On the mountain summits, where the snow clings precariously, thin sheets of ice have chiselled the peaks to ever finer points (right). Then, from as high as 24,000 feet, where enough ice and snow have accumulated, glaciers have gouged out the rock. Inching down the valleys to some 4,000 feet below the snowline, they have broadened the profiles from a narrow "V", carved by prehistoric rivers, to a smooth-based "U".

Though apparently inert, glaciers actually move at a steady pace, partly by slipping and sliding and partly by a form of plastic motion deep beneath their surface. As snow accumulates, its star-shaped crystals are compressed into rounded granules of ice. As successive layers build up to a depth of several thousands of feet, the pressure of their weight causes the lower levels slowly to flow. This "plastic" core of the glacier drags with it the brittle surface layers. The layers do not move uniformly, however, because their edges are slowed by friction with the valley walls. Wracked by different rates of flow, the edges of the glacier-ribbon continually split into crevasses and reform when the stresses diminish.

As the glacier travels, it bites into the rock over which it travels. At its head, it scoops out an armchair-shaped *cirque*. On Mt. Everest —as on many high peaks—a ring of *cirques* progressively sharpens the mountain's outline.

As the glacier moves down the valley, grinding debris from the floor and walls, it may be joined by tributaries. Because the trunk glacier usually gouges its valley at a faster rate and digs deeper, the tributaries are left "hanging", linked to the main glacier by steep ice-falls.

Glaciers transport most of the rock debris deep within, but some debris accumulates on the surface, in fringing bands called lateral moraines. When glaciers converge, these moraines meet in the centre of the trunk glacier, colouring it like a striped monster.

Most Himalayan glaciers are two to three miles long but the longest, the Siachen, gouges a 45-mile-long valley through the eastern Karakorams. Where they end, their meltwaters expose jumbles of debris in terminal moraines, where mosses and grasses may eventually take root.

Towering more than 23,000 feet near the western face of Everest, Mt. Pumori has been sculpted by ice into a near-perfect pyramid. High on the peak, melting snow has percolated behind the rock faces. In freezing as ice and expanding, it has acted like a giant chisel, exerting pressures of up to nearly one ton per square inch to split off the outer rock. At the base, where enough snow has accumulated, glaciers have gouged out cirques.

High on the Nepal-Tibet frontier, a maze of crevasses scars the surface of glacial ice in Everest's Western Cwm (Welsh: "valley"). This valley-sized cirque, carved westwards from Everest by the Khumbu Glacier, was named by the British explorer, George Mallory, apparently as an expression of his affection for the Welsh highlands. Here, as the glacier curves towards Mt. Pumori (background), it is wracked by stresses that crack open its left-hand edge.

At the head of the 2,000-foot ice-fall that joins the Western Cwm with the Khumbu Glacier, seasonal layers of winter and monsoonal snow are cleft by fissures up to 50 feet deep. Once fractured, the firmly packed snow may be weakened by weathering, causing it to collapse into a mass of icy debris.

In the Hindu Kush, the cumbrous mass of an unnamed glacier grinds an ever-widening passage through the Warm Pass. Heaving over an uneven floor, its surface has been rent by a crevasse whose nearside lip has subsided to a depth of 50 feet. Past glacial action has hollowed the flanks of the distant peaks.

Jumbled morainic debris marks the slow
retreat of the Lantang Glacier in
northern Nepal. The glacier once filled
the valley, fanning out to a point just
beyond the foreground of this
photograph. The melting ice exposed a
ridged terminal moraine, part of which
is visible (right). As the glacier's load
of ice diminished with a progressively
warmer climate, the snout retreated,
exposing less debris each warm season.

The rounded outlines of the Khung Khola Valley in northern Nepal bear witness to the shaping power of a vanished glacier. Skirting the jagged ridge (centre background), the glacier planed smooth the contours of the valley, depositing debris in hollows in the walls and floor. A dry stream bed now meanders towards lower ground and sedges and grasses emerge from soil-filled gaps between the rocks.

2/ In the Giant's Shadow

Far higher in the sky than imagination dared to suggest, a prodigious white fang—an excrescence from the jaw of the world—the summit of Everest appeared.

GEORGE LEIGH MALLORY QUOTED BY CAPTAIN JOHN NOEL/ *THROUGH TIBET TO EVEREST*

According to legend, an official of the Indian Trigonometrical Survey burst into the office of his superior in New Delhi one day in 1852 and exclaimed: "Sir, I have discovered the highest mountain in the world." In fact, the discovery was less dramatic. It was the final product of laborious cross-checking of figures from the field-survey. At the time, and for almost a century afterwards, Nepal was closed to Europeans, and the height of its major peaks could be calculated only from the Indian hills, nearly 100 miles away, by dragging up heavy surveying equipment on poles slung between two men. Their measurements were remarkably accurate. Everest was said to be 29,002 feet high. The latest recalculation, in 1953-5, gives its height as 29,028 feet (plus or minus 0.8 feet, a nice qualification, for it is the depth of a single fall of snow).

Everest, before 1852, was unknown to Westerners because it was inaccessible, and all but its peak was hidden from the Indian plains by its giant neighbours Lhotse and Nuptse. In 1848 Joseph Dalton Hooker, looking westwards from a spur of Kangchenjunga, had had a glimpse of it: "There was no continuous snowy chain; the Himalayas seemed suddenly to decline into black and rugged peaks, till in the far north-west it rose again in a white mountain mass of stupendous elevation at 80 miles distance, called by my Nepal people, 'Tsungau'."

The name Tsungau does not reappear in history. The newly discovered peak was known for several years by its code-number XV in the survey-book, and it was not until 1865 that Sir Andrew Waugh, Director of the Indian Survey, suggested that it should be called after his great predecessor, Sir George Everest, Surveyor-General of India from 1830 to 1843. Everest is the only mountain in the entire range that bears the name of an individual. When it was proposed that K2 in the Karakorams should be named after Colonel H. H. Godwin Austen who surveyed its glaciers, the suggestion displeased both the Indian Survey and the Royal Geographical Society, and was not officially adopted. There have been second thoughts even about Everest. Shortly after its christening, the Tibetan name Chomolungma was discovered, and it has been proposed as more suitable for a mountain that had been venerated under that name for centuries before Sir George Everest's was known. Some scholars, however, say that Chomolungma refers to the whole group of peaks in that area, not to Everest alone. For that reason, and also for its subsequent fame, Everest is likely to remain unchanged as the name of the highest elevation upon the earth.

A view of Everest is today easy to come by. The approach to it from the lowlands of Nepal is normally made by aeroplane. Terry Spencer and I accomplished in an hour the approach journey that took the Everest expeditions 17 days; in the season of our visit over 6,000 people made the four-day trek northwards from the airstrip at Lukla to the base-camp at the foot of the Khumbu ice-fall below Everest. There is even a Japanese-run hotel on a spur just north of Namche Bazar, the main Sherpa village of the Khumbu region. From it, we could retrace through field-glasses every agonizing footstep taken by Edmund Hillary and Tenzing Norgay up the last 2,000 feet of Everest to its summit.

But Everest is not humbled by its present-day conveniences, any more than it was diminished by surrendering to the British expedition in 1953 the blue riband of inaccessibility. It still exacts its penalties: from the mountaineer, death; from the mere trekker, mountain-sickness and a hard slog up steep paths and glacial moraines. Everest is terrifyingly eternal, and we are mortal. More than 20 men have reached its summit, but at what price in human life and suffering! The ascent becomes no easier, except psychologically, because it has been done before. There is a remoteness about this peak that must be measured by a scale more subtle than mere altitude. It stands aloof, stern rather than beautiful, graceless even, and, if one can attribute to a mass of rock the antithesis of the feeling it arouses, contemptuous. Nobody has ever loved Everest as they might love Nanda Devi, the giant of the Indian Himalayas. "It is a place," one early mountaineer remarked, "to have been to; not to go to."

Peaks of the Everest chain, swathed in snow, present the world's most spectacular horizon as they jut massively above the humble Nepalese foothills. The distant triangular peak on the left is Mount Everest (29,028 feet), the highest mountain on earth. Running in front of it is the Nuptse ridge (25,850 feet) and to its right is Lhotse (27,890 feet). The high peak at right is Makalu (27,790), first scaled in 1955.

We flew up for a closer look at the mountain in a light aeroplane piloted by an adventurous Swiss who was determined to display to best advantage not only his skill but the mountains to which he was accredited. Flying east from Kathmandu over the rumpled foothills, we saw the few roads around the Nepalese capital drop away, then the houses, then the terraced fields. As we turned north up the valley of the Dudh Kosi River, the classic approach to Everest, we found it surprisingly regular, both in gradient and direction, a straight cleft rising steadily between brown hills. I watched the altimeter climb, 15,000, 16,000, 18,000 feet. The pilot handed me his oxygen mask, and I took a few gulps, though I didn't feel I needed them yet. Suddenly we found ourselves above the snow-line, and the pilot pointed ahead:

"Everest!"

At first I was not sure which it was. We were in an amphitheatre of peaks, one poised with astonishing precariousness (it turned out to be Ama Dablam), others level with our wings. But as the direction of flight was north and Everest lies northernmost at the head of the valley, it could only be the black pyramid I saw rising clear above the rock wall that closed the upper end. It was. I was disappointed that so little of it was visible, and what there was did not conform to my notion of supremacy. It looked almost shy. The pilot pointed out other landmarks: Namche Bazar; Thyangboche Monastery, neat on its saddle-spur. These names, so familiar from newspaper accounts of the great expeditions, achieved sudden substance in such small huddles.

Terry Spencer, sitting behind me, was busy taking photographs from the cabin door which he had opened above a 10,000-foot drop, insisting that nothing, not even a sheet of clear plastic, should come between his lens and the astounding view. We flew to the top of the valley—a mosquito among wedding-cakes—and circled in a huge parabola (to use up our overload of petrol, the pilot explained, but we suspected him of being a man who took pleasure in giving pleasure), allowing us a closer look at Lhotse's ice-wall. I watched him anxiously as he floated the aircraft away from it with a falcon's ease. Then we returned down the valley towards Namche's landing-strip. It was a joke of an air-strip, the highest in the world, a finger held out waist-high by a mountain on which we took our chance to perch.

When you step suddenly on to ground 12,000 feet above sea-level, you expect to feel different. We had been warned of the effects of altitude, and heard that the Japanese hotel had oxygen on tap for those who needed it. I took my first few steps as if I was walking on a newly frozen

Like a vast watchtower, Mount Everest stands on the borders of Tibet and Nepal. Clustered around it are many of the Himalayas' greatest peaks; all those rising above 20,000 feet are marked on the map of the Everest region (right). Between the mountains flow long glaciers and rivers (shown blue), cutting their way down thousands of feet, southwards towards the Indian plains.

TIBET
NEPAL

Nangpa La
18,753 ft.

Cho Oyu
26,749 ft.

Gyachung Kang
25,991 ft.

Rongbuk Glacier

East Rongbuk Glacier

Nup La
19,636 ft. West Rongbuk Glacier

Khartaphu
23,720 ft.

Karma Changri
20,560 ft.

Lingtren Nup
20,866 ft.

Pumori
Glacier

Lingtren
21,972 ft.

Changtse
24,770 ft.

Kartse
21,350 ft.

Lungsampa Glacier

Sumna Glacier

Chumbu
22,483 ft.

Pumori
23,442 ft.

Khumbutse
21,785 ft.

Lho La
19,705 ft.

LUNAK

Ngojumba Glacier

Ice
fall

Western Cwm Glacier

Mount Everest
29,028 ft.

Kangshung Glacier

Lobujya West
20,161 ft.

Lobujya
Glacier

Khumbu Glacier

Nuptse
25,850 ft.

South Col
26,200 ft.

Lhotse
27,890 ft.

"Peak 38"
24,898 ft.

Pethangtse
22,014 ft.

Lobujya East
20,075 ft.

LOBUJYA

Lhotse Shar
27,503 ft.

TIBET
NEPAL

Kyajo Ri
20,295 ft.

Nuptse Glacier

Lhotse Glacier

"Island Peak"
20,305 ft.

Cho Polu
22,093 ft.

Chago
22,590 ft.

Makalu II
25,130 ft.

Bhote Kosi

Cholatse
21,129 ft.

Taweche
20,889 ft.

PHERICHE

DINGBOCHE

CHUKHUNG

Ama
Dablam
Glacier

Baruntse
23,688 ft.

Barun Glacier

Makalu
27,790 ft.

Langmoche Khola

PANGBOCHE

Imja Khola

Ama Dablam
22,493 ft.

Hongu Glacier

Thami Khola

THYANGBOCHE

"Peak 4"
22,047 ft.

Dudh Kosi

NAMCHE BAZAR

Hongu South Peak
20,013 ft.

"Pyramid Peak"
22,430 ft.

Teng Kangpoche
21,325 ft.

Kwangde
20,299 ft.

Thamserku
21,680 ft.

Kangtega
21,932 ft.

Hongu Khola

"Peak 41"
21,830 ft.

Chamlang
24,012 ft.

Dudh Kosi

Kyangshar Khola

"Peak 43"
22,208 ft.

Karyolung
21,920 ft.

Mera
21,120 ft.

LUKLA

0   2   4   6   8   10
MILES

pond. It was quite unnecessary. I felt exhilarated or light-headed more than breathless, and suffered nothing more than a slight headache.

Later that day we took a more prolonged look at our exalted surroundings. The Dudh Kosi Valley was an amazing sight. Mist swam into it from each end, changing its shape and colour every half-minute. Downwards, towards the plain, the hills descended in flying buttresses, matching each other on both sides of the river, while northwards they broke into the peaks of the great snow-mountains. Ama Dablam, as I had noticed from the air, was dominant because it stands alone, its head nodding seemingly in defiance of the law of gravity. To the north was the *bombe glacée* of Taweche, and alongside us a graceful mountain of which I had never previously heard, Kangtega (21,932 feet), rising in lacey *arêtes* to a summit fluted by ice-furrows. A cloud broke its outline at mid-point. Mountains like this need clouds to assert their height, and a cloud's movement to emphasize their stability. I have seen the Himalayas, cloud-free at dawn, lose all their colour and majesty, looking like Swiss replicas of themselves. They need clouds for the same reason that emperors need robes and trappings.

Ahead was Everest. Now I could focus field-glasses on its crest. In the wonderfully clear air every detail of its structure was visible, black rocks lightly streaked with snow, rising in ribs to form a tent-like summit. From this vantage point there was no sign of its culminating snow-dome, on to which Hillary had cut the final steps "with a few whacks of the ice-axe". But there was the south summit, notching the skyline a little lower down; and there the 40-foot step of rock that so nearly defeated him in the last hour of his ascent. The base of the summit-triangle was cut off just above the South Col by Nuptse's battlemented crest, scarcely deserving to be named a mountain in its own right, I thought resentfully; but at its far end rose Lhotse, proud and positive. The sun was setting. Heavy clouds drifted across the crimson cloth of Nuptse's wall. The colours were those of a Turner painting: first, strawberry streaked with cream, changing into a dying fire as rapidly as Terry could capture it, and finally into amber. As the snow-slopes lost the sun, only the peaks blazed out, like candles, to be extinguished one by one. Everest's was the last to go, as if to proclaim in this unmistakable manner that it was, in fact, supreme.

It might be imagined that so great a barrier as Everest and its satellites is impenetrable except by the most intrepid mountaineers. But the Everest group, like all others in the Himalayas, is bordered by passes on each side, and men have crossed them immemorially for trade and cultural exchange. The Sherpas came south by these routes in the Middle Ages, and within very recent times double their number of Tibetan refugees. In the reverse direction, the Nepalese have climbed the passes to barter their goods and skills in Tibetan markets. The frontier has been closed to foreigners since 1950, when the Chinese occupied Tibet, but trade, now mostly in smuggled goods, still goes on.

The Sherpas form a tiny tribe of a few thousand people, unknown and cut off by the mountains until some few years ago, and now world-symbols for good-natured endurance. Trade and mountain-porterage have given them a higher standard of living than their neighbours to the south, and their religion is a source of joy evident in their courtesy and creased smiles. "Compassion with all animate creatures," wrote C. F. Haimendorf, the eminent anthropologist, who knows them best, "is in their eyes the essence of human virtue;" and creatures include man. These are the people, Mongol by origin, Nepalese by adoption, who have chosen to inhabit one of the most intractable corners of the globe.

Namche Bazar itself is at the junction of the Dudh Kosi with a lateral valley that leads to the frontier pass of Nangpa La, over 18,000 feet above sea-level. The outside world has already left its mark on Namche since the first European entered it in 1950. There is now a school, a police-post, several open-fronted shops selling beer and canned peaches to the trek-kers, and touching hand-painted notices advertising "restaurants" and "hotels" that turn out to be little more than invitations to share a family's meal and the mat-covered bedstead in their only room. In essence, how-ever, the character of the village is unchanged. It has its air-strip high above, but no road; and a squat temple, with a stream of clear water flowing past it, as it always had. The village street opens into a small piazza where yak-wool is spun and woven into carpets. Prayer-flags flutter over every house, and the inscription that they carry, *Om mane padme hum* ("Hail to the jewel in the lotus") is endlessly repeated in paint or carving on prominent rocks. There is a mood of propitiation in these hills. In the small chapel, the wall-paintings depicted the Himalayas euphemistically as the size of the Apennines in Italian primitives.

Next day we began walking towards Everest, with a Sherpa to carry our camera equipment. We walked the Thyangboche path, 2,000 feet down to the bed of the Dudh Kosi, to get the feel of the mountains and to acclimatize. The path is steep, but it was easy walking on the way down, rubber soles cupping the strewn stones, and the path led through delightful country, across sloping meadows and through groves of

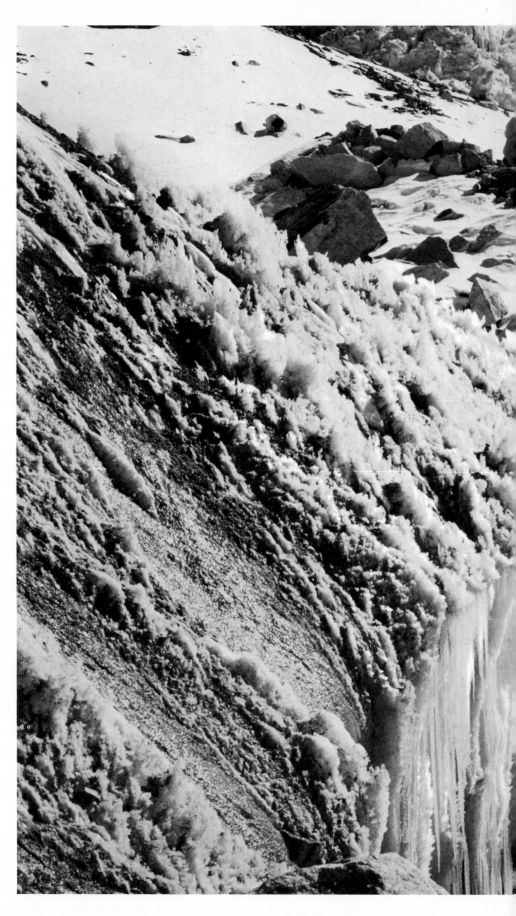

Icicles hang in a heavy curtain across the Khumbu Glacier, west of Everest. The curtain—like the rest of the glacier surface that is littered here with morainic debris of pebbles and boulders—is in a constant state of change and motion. Within days, or perhaps even hours, the melting of the ice and the irregular movement of the glacier will have obliterated the curtain and the crevasse below it.

twisted juniper and birch dripping with pale green lichen. The Dudh Kosi was white with constant turmoil and its granite boulders shone with specks of mica. (Hence its name, Dudh Kosi which means "Milk River.") When suspended in great cliffs, the rock is almost indistinguishable from blocks of ice.

So this stream was the collected outpouring of the Everest massif! It seemed unexpectedly small; but then I remembered that snow does not fall thickly at great heights, and most of what does fall is eternally retained there if it is not blown away or burnt off by evaporation before it melts. A bridge crosses the river at this point, and as we sat beside it, a team of yaks picked its way across—heavy, hairy oxen, that combine the rôles of porters and domestic cattle, supplying the mountain people with milk and the soft wool of their bellies for the weaving of blankets and many items of clothing.

From the river the path zig-zags up to the Thyangboche spur, on which an aging Buddhist monk was moved in the 1920s to build a monastery facing the most dramatic backdrop in the world, and beyond it Tibet, the source of his inspiration. An earthquake destroyed the buildings in 1934 and the abbot died from the shock a few weeks later, aged 85. But it was soon rebuilt by his successor, who now presides over a community of some 40 lamas. The small compound is almost the last inhabited locality on the Everest route. The main channel of the Dudh Kosi breaks northwest to collect the water of Cho Oyu, and a relatively minor torrent called the Imja Khola leads up the moraine of the Khumbu Glacier. The route, though now well-trodden, is appropriately barren. It is easy walking, since the glacial debris provides a firm footing and the upward slope is gradual. But the way is long and the nights sharp with frost, and the rising altitude cuts every gulp of air in half.

The base-camp lies at nearly 18,000 feet, at the foot of the Khumbu ice-fall. There is no feature on the approach to a mountain more familiar than this. The majority of us who enjoy our mountaineering vicariously, by reading about it, tend to skip lower ordeals and are only interested in the summit. With Everest it is different. Its features are as familiar to us as our own favourite park. The ice-fall, the Western Cwm, the south-west face. the Lhotse wall, the South Col, the south summit, are milestones on a journey that we have taken in the imagination many times: those of an older generation will add the Rongbuk Glacier and the North Col from memories of pre-war expeditions. But the greatest of all is the ice-fall, because it is infinitely spectacular and dangerous. It looks like the ruins of a great city encased in ice and slowly subsiding down a chute 2,000 feet high. It is composed of vast blocks of ice-masonry—towers and walls and pinnacles—all of which must eventually topple as the steady pressure of the glacier above it forces the whole cracking mass forwards and downwards. It is the ladder by which all expeditions mount to the platform from which the summit must be scaled; but it is a ladder with rotten rungs. It is never the same from one hour to the next; never stable; never silent. A sudden rattle, and down comes an ice-tower: a deep sigh, and a crevasse opens. The ice-fall separates men from boys, mountaineers from tourists.

Beyond and above it lies the great snow-bath of the Western Cwm, formed by Nuptse on one side, by Everest's own south-west face on the other, and by Lhotse at the far end. It is a long, slow drag across it to the base of the encircling walls, and then Everest makes its third, or fourth, beginning, for it is a mountain that must be divided not into chapters, but into volumes. Snow and ice give place to bare rock. Skills that would be regarded as commonplace in Snowdonia or the Appalachians must now be exercised in the teeth of a 100 m.p.h. gale, a temperature drop to −40°F, and an altitude that makes a man catch each breath with pain. The actual danger is not so great, once the ice-fall has been surmounted. It is the attrition of weeks of bitter cold and wind that eventually wears down the strongest men.

Everest has a character quite different from that of any other mountain. It would be disappointing if it were like its neighbour Cho Oyu, only 2,000 feet lower and according to Chris Bonington, who led the British Everest expedition in 1972, "little more than a very high-altitude fell walk"; or Nuptse, which never makes up its mind to be a mountain at all. Everest is formidably masculine and certain, a giant who knows his rights. But there is a special grace, too, in the long sweeps of ice and rock that mitigates its extreme aloofness. I gazed at it with admiration, regretting that because its peak marks a sealed frontier, I would never be able to see its far side, by all accounts even more stupendous.

NATURE WALK /Through Kali Gandaki Gorge

PHOTOGRAPHS BY TERENCE SPENCER

The valley of the Kali Gandaki in central Nepal is said to be the deepest gorge in the world. It separates two of the world's largest mountain massifs—Dhaulagiri and Annapurna—each of which has a main peak of over 26,000 feet. The distance between them is 22 miles, and the bed of the river at its central point lies 18,500 feet below.

But the word gorge needs some qualification: it suggests a narrow slit cut by a river between vertical rock walls. The Kali Gandaki certainly has its dramatic passages, but much of its upper course, carved by glaciers in the remote past, is a mile wide, and its banks, though sometimes extremely precipitous, are more often gently inclined. No road runs along it, but there is a path that can be followed from village to village by men and pack-animals, and it has been known for centuries to pilgrims, traders and migrant families as one of the easiest breaches of the Himalayan chain.

The Kali Gandaki claims another distinction. Its upper part is a "dry" valley. The monsoon exhausts itself against the southern slopes, and although rain or at least humid mist can creep along the mountain walls, it does not penetrate the valley floor. A dessicating wind blowing from the south dries it still further, and the increasing altitude completes the process. The valley becomes a semi-desert, spotted with spiny shrub, only 20 miles beyond the point where its vegetation is riotously tropical. In the space of a day's march one can descend from the sharp dry sunshine and wind-blown Tibetan flora around the village of Jomosom to the steamy humidity and sub-tropical monsoon flora of the gorges below the village of Ghasa. The abruptness of the change is astonishing.

Terry Spencer and I took four days to cover the length of the gorge. He with cameras, I with notebook, walked those 20 miles in the month of November, when the monsoon finally ended and sparkling sun irradiated unsullied snow.

As we flew from Kathmandu we swung north up the valley that we were to descend on foot and could pick out the thin silver chain of the Kali Gandaki River snaking between the two vast mountains. We landed at Jomosom on sand and gravel, at an altitude of 9,000 feet, 20 miles from the nearest point in Tibet, and were met by the seven porters whom we had engaged to carry our tents

TOWERING WALLS DWARF A TRAIL ALONG THE KALI GANDAKI GORGE

and stores during the coming trek.

As we took our first steps away from the airstrip, we noticed at once that the mountain slopes were treeless until some 2,500 feet above the valley floor, and there a few birches drifted hesitantly across them, encouraged by the last flicker of the forked monsoon rainfall.

GANDAKI AT ITS WIDEST

Looking north towards the Mustang district, we saw that even these few wanderers gave up the struggle, and the ground was quite barren.

Terry and I did not stay with the porters, for they remained on the path while we hurried from one dramatic scene to another, making notes and taking photographs. The valley floor swelled in humps like dunes, but there were patches of

SEMI-DESERT LAND

they do not approach each other too closely. If they do, a twist of the wings and a sharp turn to left or right avoids a collision and harmony is once more restored.

We crossed the river, a tumbling torrent grey with cold, and made our way up the east slopes to a small lake that I had spotted from the aeroplane. Tiny balls of cloud hung in the sky, as if they had been fired there by anti-aircraft guns. Every sound was audible from a mile away, the chinking of shod boots against a stone, the bells of a distant donkey team, and somewhere a woman was singing in the quavering fashion of the East. Growing out of the bank of a small tributary of the Gandaki was a birch with tawny leaves—the first splash of colour we had seen—and its branches leaned in a graceful curve towards the open riverbed. They had yielded to the persistent wind that we were soon to experience.

Below the Snow Kingdom

An hour later we reached the lake, a silver salver dropped flat between the mountains and crumpled at its edges. The hillside above it was streaked with bright streams carrying the melting snow from the surrounding peaks. The summit of Dhaulagiri I was always visible. Through binoculars I could walk it in imagination so clear was the air. A mattress of snow 50 feet thick lay on a ridge above its glacier, poised to collapse in a soft smothering avalanche. These gigantic forces have a gentle way (gentle, it seemed, from that distance) of restoring

vegetation that stained the sterile sweeps of sand: scattered pincushions of caragana, another creeping plant barely recognizable as a thwarted honeysuckle, and bushy junipers that lower down the valley I was to see growing to 50 feet. This was semi-desert. Wind-borne particles had carved the valley walls into fluted cliffs down which sheep and yaks picked their way to the water in the riverbed. The Tibetan plateau is said to be the only region of the earth's surface where desert and arctic conditions coexist; and you will not find the next forest to the north for another 2,000 miles, in the wasteland of Siberia.

High in the sky cranes, storks and eagles glide over Jomosom on thermals. The birds are at ease as long as

TAWNY-LEAVED BIRCH

SUMMIT OF DHAULAGIRI

soil onto the rocks and whipping it into delicately spiralled patterns. Pools of water at my feet were imprisoned by a scattering of loose stones and edged by crackling ice.

Then a yard away on the ground I saw an ammonite. This, I knew, was evidence that the mountains were raised up from parts of what had once been the sea-bed between India and northern Asia like a primordial Atlantis in reverse. However, our first day was closing in on us. In failing light and increasing cold, our porters erected our tents and fed us a warming meal of mutton, carrots and cauliflower, and tea laced with rum. We felt very content as, wrapped in all our spare clothing to keep out the cold, we crawled into our sleeping bags.

their equilibrium: a puff of snow and a million tons find a new level; and then the process begins again.

But the peace of the scene was illusory. A plume of snow flying from the summit indicated freezing gales up there, and we were told that a British expedition had been six weeks aloft, struggling to climb the last 2,000 feet of Dhaulagiri IV. Two men, we later heard, an Englishman and a Sherpa, were killed, and the others withdrew defeated, like nine expeditions before them. The fourth peak of Dhaulagiri—that companion of our easy walk, that enemy of their brutal climb—remains unconquered.

The wind began to rise predictably at noon, a strong funnelling of cool air from the south, blowing sandy

FOSSIL AMMONITE

We were tired and the night passed quickly. When we woke at 6 a.m., after 11 hours' darkness, the sun was breaking over the eastern crests. The crisp freshness of the new day was inspiring—off came the anorak, off the sweater and we could stride the moraines in exultation before breakfast.

By 7 a.m. we were on our way. I

SAND BLOWN ON TO ROCK

was scarcely aware of losing height as we walked, until I glanced down at the tumbling river; and walking was very easy along the flats of the widening valley or on a narrow path cut from the cliff walls. Down a side valley a glacier of mud had carried whole tree trunks from the upper levels. Here, too, was more evidence of the uplifted sea-bed that became the Himalayas. A great boulder striped with orange was calcium carbonate—the consolidated remains of sea animals.

A black juniper came down to the valley floor at the village of Tukche, and in a sheltered corner stood a bush with orange berries: *Hippophae*, the buckthorn. Here the country began to change perceptibly. Along the ridges from the south strode the advance guard of an army of conifers: the east Himalayan fir,

CALCIUM CARBONATE ROCK

Abies spectabilis, and its more common neighbour, the Bhutan pine, *Pinus wallichiana*, a magnificent tree of gleaming colour and beautiful texture.

The path climbed again along the cliff-face towards Larjung, where we were to make our second camp, and we looked down on a string of donkeys crossing the valley floor—microscopic reminders of the scale of the breach we were following. At Larjung we found a pleasant field near the river, where we ate before wrapping ourselves up against the cold of night. We could hear dogs barking loudly in the village.

Life in High Forests

In the morning, we rose refreshed, exhilarated by the prospect of the day's march. This was to be the day when we crossed into the splendours of tropical Kali Gandaki. We set off in perfect walking weather, the sun shining above us. Although the gorge was still wide and the river was still comparatively small within it, there was now an urgency about its passage and it seemed to share our enthusiasm to reach greener pastures ahead. Even the vegetation closed in on it so that it appeared to run more directly towards its goal. Thick forests of pine clung to the valley slopes and also to the riverbed itself. The river soon narrowed to its first gorge, where the yellow spike of *Gynura cusimbua*, grew in profusion among the pines. Ice Age glaciers had not penetrated this far, and the passage of the Kali Gandaki farther south was left to its own

GYNURA CUSIMBUA

SUB-TROPICAL KALI GANDAKI GORGE

GRIFFON VULTURE

SILHOUETTED RAVENS

erosive powers. The drop in altitude —we had now come down to 4,800 feet—the growing influence of the monsoon and melting snows were collectively responsible for the lusher vegetation that now began to surround us. With the encroaching flowers and the evergreen came birds, insects and small reptiles and amphibians. None of them was numerous for they were hidden. In the surrounding forest, I was later told, we must have passed a hundred species of birds, but they were silent and reluctant to rise above tree-height. But we did see Himalayan griffon vultures and ravens. The former is a powerful scavenger and it sailed over the valley, its keen eyes scanning the ground for a decaying carcass. The ravens, among the largest members of the crow family, performed remarkable aerial contortions around high precipices. But of the lovely flycatchers and the laughing thrushes of the Himalayas there was no sign.

Before the village of Ghasa we had lunch overlooking a splendid waterfall. It was 50 feet high, a huge, black slab of smooth rock down which a narrow trickle of water made its way. We could easily imagine the volume of water that must come cascading over this ridge during the full force of the monsoon rains. In the afternoon we made little progress, fearing for our lives as we walked the steep and stony paths with an almost precipitous drop on one side. We stopped at Kobre and shared a field with some cattle. It was a depressing campsite, but the welcome night warmth enabled us to sleep loosely clad, cradled on pine needles.

In the morning sunlight flooded the valley and we set off through our first rhododendron forest. Its trees grew to 40 feet and their twisted brown branches were hung with lichen—an isolated jungle among the stateliness of the pines.

SHEER WATERFALL

One of the porters brought us a miraculous creature. The birds and mammals may have been hidden, but he had found a huge praying mantis. The extraordinary monster-insect sat frozen on a rock, hoping by its immobility to avoid detection. It must be among the most delicately formed of all creatures, I thought, with its long spidery legs and twig-thin fuselage. Strangest of all is its head. It is lifted from legend, from nightmares, peering with fixed eyes, tremulous with antennae, aggressive in aspect and intent, but so vulnerable that its dragon-like features seemed absurd.

Torrential Waters

We walked on past Ghasa. The stands of chir and pines were touched by the sun, pale green, dark green. A white *Delias* butterfly sailed past us and settled momentarily on a little flowerhead. It closed its wings and revealed a shock of bright red and yellow on

RHODODENDRON GROVE

PRAYING MANTIS

DELIAS BUTTERFLY

their underside—enough to frighten any predator, I thought—before it launched itself into the air again.

Now the water of the main river was whipped into a sudden frenzy and poured with demonic force through two narrow channels each side of a boulder. Lower down the scene was repeated with augmented violence. Here the Gandaki strained in a final effort to carve its way between the constraining bulks of Annapurna and Dhaulagiri. From a mile wide the river was compressed into a teapot's spout, its banks forming a true gorge for a few yards at a time. Sometimes we had to climb high over its shoulders to make any progress at all.

Sub-tropical Nepal rose to meet us. Flowers and trees grew in cups of soil right down to the river's edge. We stopped to look back and saw with surprise that the great mountains were behind us. We had walked clean through the Himalayas from north to south.

GANDAKI SURGING THROUGH NARROW GORGE

3/ Predator and Prey

The Himalayas from plain to snow give shelter to such a variety of wild animals that if an Ark were to be stocked from no other source, it would preserve an élite of the animal kingdom. The richest level is the lowest, the jungle or *terai*, where are found most of the animals of children's story books or Uccello's paintings, among them the tiger, leopard, monkey, elephant, crocodile and rhinoceros. The last three do not wander far from the lowest foothills, but the others climb from the jungle in their insatiable quest for food, and come into contact and conflict with the creatures of the middle zone: the bear, the jackal, the red panda—and man. These give place to the animals of the rich grassland above the trees, the yaks and wild asses, the sheep and goats which carry an armoury of strangely contorted horns. Throughout the three zones are spread the deer, prey for the carnivores, and they, too, vary in species according to the altitude, as do the creeping creatures and the birds.

At both extremes, the severity of the struggle for existence is at its maximum; but while in the rain forest it is the struggle between one animal and another that counts, in the high mountains it is the struggle with altitude and the elements. In one case there is usually an over-abundance of food; in the other, extreme scarcity. Most animals stop where the plants stop, at about 19,000 feet. But climbers on Everest have seen the tracks of mountain sheep at 20,000 feet, of hares and foxes at 21,000, of wolves at 21,500. The birds and tiny crawling things survive highest. They alone, or some of them, would have no need to enter the Ark. Jumping spiders were found at 22,000 feet by the 1924 Everest expedition. Neither freaks nor wanderers, they have since been shown to be part of a small but hardy community in permanent residence. Here, in the lofty wastes, the predatory instinct that governs life on the forested slopes reasserts itself. To survive, the spiders feed on spring-tails, insects one-fifth of an inch long, which derive their name from a trigger-like mechanism under their bodies capable of throwing them a few inches into the air. These feed, in their turn, on the detritus of the lower slopes, blown upwards by the wind: pollen, dead flies, rotting leaf fragments and the young of various insects and spiders that disperse by rising on a "parachute" of thread, and drift with the wind.

At such heights the cold is always intense. But this presents no problem for the permanent community above the snow-line. During the day the spider's dark-brown body soaks in the sun's heat and the springtail obtains warmth from the stones. Both creatures withstand drops in temperature by going into a state resembling hibernation. It is possible that in these frozen regions there exist other colonies of spiders and insects, so far unstudied because their habitat is lethal to all but the fittest of men. It may even be that insurgent life, with all the pressure of millions of years of reproduction and evolution behind it, has managed to scale the highest peaks on earth.

The realm of Himalayan fauna may be seen diagrammatically as a layered pyramid. As the seasons change, animals ascend or descend the pyramid to escape the worst of the heat or the cold, some using larger lungs to make the most of rarefied air, others equipped with sweat glands to compensate for the oven-heat of the tropical plains. Darwin would have found here within a few thousand feet concentrated proof of his theory that it is the fittest that survive.

It is, however, only in menageries, like those at Delhi or Kabul, or stuffed, glittering with glass eyes, in the lounges of hotels or airports, that one is likely to see more than a tiny proportion of these animals. All but the birds and monkeys are very shy, and many species are now extremely rare. They range over vast and thickly sheltered territories; they fear each other, with reason; they move with stealth, and their coats are camouflaged; many of them are nocturnal in their habits; others hibernate. Only in specially favoured areas like the state-protected reserves can they be seen in any numbers, or at a great distance in open country and above the trees.

By far the most ubiquitous and visible animal in the Himalayas is man, and he is slowly destroying the other spieces. The main reason is that man is in direct competition with other animals for space. To win more land for agriculture, the hill-farmers fell or burn back virgin forests, as in the Nepalese *terai*. Deprived of normal food supplies, the animals begin raiding crops and domestic livestock. In turn they are killed by farmers with livelihoods to protect. (There is no blame here: all over the Himalayan region and in every part of the civilized world the cry is raised, Protect the animals. Yet it is often overlooked that man is also an animal, and if he is in competition with other animals, his livelihood, too, deserves at least an equal degree of protection.)

Hunting and poaching also take their toll of the wild life. Tourists pay £3,000 to shoot a Marco Polo sheep, with its horns that curve into a complete circle and then sweep outwards, and only a little less for the near-extinct markhor, a goat with corkscrew horns that are often more than four feet long. The pelt of a snow-leopard can fetch £100 and the musk pod of the musk-deer—used in the manufacture of high-grade perfume—at least £1,000. Many inhabitants of the Himalayas have religious taboos against killing far more effective than any government directive, but many more have no qualms about hunting meat for the pot or snaring the valuable musk-deer. Traplines extend for miles along the slopes of the Mailung Khola River, in Central Nepal, and whole villages make their living from poaching and hunting.

Nevertheless, there are regions of the world where men and animals in their sparse numbers can co-exist. Terry Spencer and I went to one Indian reserve, a 500-square-mile tract of jungle and open grassland in the lowest of the Himalayan foothills. The experience was both thrilling and shaming. We wished to see in their natural state some of the animals that penetrate the higher hills. The game warden promised to arrange for us to photograph a tiger. Late that night he tethered a buffalo some two miles from the bungalow where we stayed, and while we ate and slept, the terrible kill took place, fortunately out of earshot. The warden confirmed in the morning that "the bait had been taken"—a nice euphemism, I thought—and the tiger was in the area. So off we went on an elephant to view the scene of the night's carnage.

From our elevated platform we could observe a world in which Adam and Eve would have felt at home. Brilliantly coloured parakeets scattered at our approach, vultures (the nastiest-looking creatures I have ever seen apart from bats) watched obscenely from the branches of dead sal trees, and several types of deer bounded from under our feet. When we came to

Frozen by the flash, two musk-deer are photographed on their nocturnal search for plant food. These rare inhabitants of the Himalayan forests are extremely shy—and with good reason. Both males and females have a gland under the tail that secretes pungent musk, a substance that is extremely valuable as a perfume base, and for which the deer are hunted and killed. Another unusual feature of the animal, evident in this photograph, is the long tusk-like canine teeth, which it uses in territorial combat and for defence.

the site of the kill, we were told to climb a wooden tower. A man with a rifle, I noticed, took up position behind us, just in case.

The beat began. Our elephant lumbered off to join five others, and, urged on by the cries of the *mahouts*, they moved away a quarter of a mile, to drive into our clearing the tiger that was supposed to be lying up in the jungle fast asleep, sated by its enormous meal. We were to remain completely quiet. Terry focused his camera on the clearing. We could see the high grass and bushes violently agitated as the elephants moved forwards. Birds began to scream across the clearing. Then came an absurd anticlimax. The elephants emerged into the open, their trunks hanging foolishly; but no tiger. The jungle was then beaten from the opposite direction, again with no result. The tiger had loped off elsewhere; the trick had been played on it once too often.

As we swayed slowly back to camp, we felt less disappointment than shame. I was actually glad not to have seen the tiger. In compensation there was evidence around us of the less ferocious life of the jungle. The chital, the loveliest of all deer, were moving in small herds, a blaze of white dots on their chestnut flanks; their duller cousins, the hog deer. roamed near by. Rhesus monkeys swung from tree to tree in play; and then, suddenly, one of the noblest beasts of the forest, a sambur, rose at a few yards' distance to stare at us—frozen by fear more than curiosity, big as a pony, its graceful antlers spread against a background of green.

We sensed fear all around us, as if every living thing was holding its breath. The jungle, at least in daytime, is a silent place. There was fear in the movements of the chital, a tentative dance of hooves preceding a sudden prance and gallop; fear in the darting eyes of the monkeys; fear in the desertion of the sambur by its mate. I wondered why they chose to inhabit a place where danger lurked so continuously, where there were 50 tigers out of the 2,000 left in the entire Indian sub-continent.

Yet, on reflection, there is a balance in this savage process that is admirable, an assurance that rich and complex ecologies can be preserved. Evolution has provided each herbivore with defences: teeth, claws, horns, thick skins, acute hearing or eyesight or sense of smell, fleetness of foot, stealth, vocal cords to give warning, camouflage for concealment, nocturnal habits, the protection of the herd. But none of these attributes is a guarantee of survival. Male antlers and horns, efficient enough weapons or deterrents against rivals of the same species, are useless against serious attack by carnivores; and the chital's bright dappled coat, excellent camouflage in broken ground, draws attention to the creature when it strays into the forest fringes. Predators, adapted to exploit any opportunity, help ensure a healthy herbivorous population, limited in number so that no strain is imposed by overgrazing on the resources of their habitat.

I asked the warden about these things. He was a likeable Indian with a great love of animals, but he described with evident admiration how a tiger kills. It can pursue its quarry for about 200 yards, and if not out-distanced, bowls it over, breaking its neck on the run. With its jaws it severs the jugular vein. Then it looks for signs of a rival that could steal its prey. If all is clear, it places one paw on its victim's shoulder, the other on the ground, and gnaws at the neck. Having tasted the meal, the tiger eviscerates the kill with a single stroke of its claws, and drags the carcass away to thicker cover, where it begins the serious eating, start-ing always with the hindquarters. The warden had witnessed this procedure many times, and it had never varied. It did not horrify him; it was "mathematical balance." If there were no deer, he argued, the vegeta-tion would grow rank: if there were no tigers, the deer would multiply so rapidly that they would destroy it all.

Man must, of course, occasionally act as executioner. When I reached the Gorapani Pass, in Nepal, I heard that only two days earlier a tiger had killed a water-buffalo in the village. When I descended the Kali Gandaki Gorge a schoolmaster told me that every summer tigers raid the neighbourhood for cattle, and the children are locked up. But control may be exercised without cruelty. In his classic, *Man Eaters of Kumaon*, Jim Corbett describes how he shot half a dozen of the most notorious killers in the very district we were visiting. One tiger had killed 434 people before it fell to Corbett's rifle. Yet he loved the tigers and leopards that he was employed to kill. He once shot a man-eater when it was asleep, and felt the need to write a whole paragraph of apology. For the tiger is not the natural enemy of man, as man is of the tiger. "It is only when tigers have been incapacitated through wounds or old age," Corbett writes, "that, in order to live, they are compelled to take to a diet of human flesh"—presumably because men are less agile in escaping than deer. Corbett spent 32 years in the pursuit of carnivores, "and though I have seen sights which would cause a stone to weep, I have not seen a case where the tiger has been deliberately cruel, or killed more than was necessary to satisfy its hunger or its cubs".

Of the leopards he wrote: "Those who have never seen a leopard under favourable conditions in his natural surroundings can have no conception of the grace of movement and beauty of colouring of this most graceful and beautiful of all animals.... To class such an animal as

Its plumed ears alert, a lynx pads warily through the Upper Indus Valley in search of deer, which it kills with a single bite to the neck.

vermin, as is done in some parts of India, is a crime which only those could perpetrate whose knowledge is limited to the miserable, underfed and mangy specimens seen in captivity." It is the most convincing argument for preservation that I have read anywhere. Supreme in the development of tooth and claw, in grace, strength and agility, in sight, sense, hearing and the craft of hunting, and with an intelligence surpassed only by that of man and the higher apes, the great cats of the jungle are masterpieces of creation, and should not in any circumstances that I can imagine be eliminated from it.

Tigers and leopards are rarities, and I saw none. Nor did I see in the wild any of the smaller cats that have found a home in the Himalayas. They include the leopard cat, only two feet long, a miniature panther that preys on small birds and mammals, sleeps in tree hollows, and is seen, though rarely, from plain level up to 9,000 feet; the jungle cat, about the same size as a domestic cat, which prefers drier and more open ground, and is found quite commonly near the villages of Kashmir; the lynx, a little larger, and possessing the proverbial eyesight and hearing of its European and Canadian cousins, which frequents the Upper Indus Valley as high as 11,000 feet; and, oddest of all, the fishing cat, an inhabitant of heavy jungle, which can scoop up fish from the water with its paw and has been known to attack sheep and even children.

I did, however, see troops of monkeys at the most unexpected places—by the roadside, on bridge parapets, and in a thicket between two Nepalese villages that was so small that it was more like a playground than serious cover. They are the tamest of untamed animals, and have been known in India to throng the platforms of railway stations awaiting passenger trains from which to pilfer discarded sandwiches. Two species of monkey predominate in the lower Himalayas up to 8,000 feet; the rhesus and the langur. Of the two, the rhesus is the uglier, with its frowning face and red behind. The langurs are supremely graceful and have endearing little faces and very long tails. Each is endowed with amazing agility in trees and on the ground, using spindly branches to catapult itself up to 30 feet, seldom misjudging the distance or the capacity of a branch to bear its flung weight. At other times they are still, or relatively still, for no monkey out of the scores I watched remained quite motionless for a second. They were catching at leaves, nibbling at shoots, darting glances from side to side, or picking at their fur, not, as is generally supposed, for vermin, for monkeys are remarkably free from them, but for minute burrs or pieces of loose skin. (At other times mutual

A red panda, or cat-bear, browses through the mountain forest in search of leaves and fruit. In fact a member of the racoon family with only superficial similarities to cat and bear, the red panda leads a mostly arboreal existence at altitudes between 7,000 and 12,000 feet. It sleeps in trees for most of the day, feeding at ground level in the early morning and evening. Its toy-like appearance is deceptive. The panda has razor-sharp claws and a vicious bite.

social grooming takes place.) Their wide range of facial expression and vocal calls and their companionableness towards each other and to man make them the Pucks of the forest. But they also are prey. A leopard can seize a monkey from a tree by a quick lunge and scramble, and if a python traps one in its coils, the monkey has no chance. Unlike the baboon, it has never learnt to use a stick or stone as a weapon of defence.

From foothills to mountain peaks live the bears, three different species of them, each to its own altitude. The sloth bear inhabits the foothills, the black bear prefers the lower forested slopes, and the immense brown bear dwells on the open peaks above the tree-line. Although none of them is entirely carnivorous, feeding mainly on grass, roots and insects, all are potentially dangerous to man and are feared by the natives more than any other animal, except possibly the wild dogs. If disturbed they can break into a lumbering gallop and rear up in a terrifying manner. They kill, not by hugging, but by striking, and their great claws can inflict terrible wounds. The sloth bear, which can grow up to six feet and weigh 250 pounds, is particularly dangerous because of its poor vision and hearing. Approached from downwind, it will not be aware of an interloper until he is almost on top of it. Then, in a panic, the sloth bear will charge, knocking its enemy flat and mauling him before rushing off.

The black bear, however, which may grow to five feet and weigh up to 500 pounds, shows little fear of man and sometimes descends to raid crops. Some members of the species also acquire a taste for flesh and the black bear has been cited as one of the main predators on the Kashmir stag. Its most unusual talent is curling up in a ball and rolling downhill. On the open slopes above the tree-line, the brown bear, which can grow to over nine feet and weigh as much as 650 pounds, avoids contact with man and is rarely seen.

Both black and brown bears hibernate during the winter, in caves or nooks of trees. All their bodily functions—digestion, heartbeat, respiration—are so greatly reduced that they emerge after four or five months almost as fat as at the start. They hibernate not in order to avoid the cold, because they can, and do, move to lower and more sheltered ground, but for lack of food. The brown bear in springtime wakes from its long sleep to follow the receding snow-line to its permanent level, where throughout the summer it lives isolated and unloved, turning over stones for voles, digging marmots from their burrows and occasionally raiding the high grazings for sheep and goats. But awake or sleeping the bear invests the forest with terror.

A more innocuous if less impressive inhabitant of Nepal, Sikkim and the mountains eastwards is the cat-bear or red panda. About the same size and shape as a fox, it is bright chestnut in colour, with a long bushy tail ringed by bars of white, and seems to have little in common with either the bear or the giant panda, whose home is the bamboo forests of south-west China. Although both pandas do have several similarities, including "sixth fingers"—pads on the front paws that help them to hold bamboo stems when feeding—and are usually classed as members of the racoon family, some zoologists doubt if they are related, asserting that the Chinese but not the Himalayan variety belongs to the bear family. Whatever its origins, it is easy to understand why the red panda makes such a popular pet. A lovely, silky little creature that pads around in a friendly way, it is as much at home in a drawing-room as in a forest.

Another creature that has become popular in the West—though few would want it in their drawing-room—is the *Yeti* or "Abominable Snowman." Robert Fleming jr., the foremost zoologist in Nepal, told me that he discounted many of the stories told about the *Yeti* as "hobgoblin legends" invented to frighten children. A Sherpa hunter of his acquaintance, with 40 years' experience of the mountains, had never seen one. "Still," Fleming concluded, "there *is* something unexplained." The porter whom we engaged was more cynical. "Only old men have seen a *Yeti*," he declared emphatically. I formed a sudden picture of garrulous dotards boasting by the fireside of an encounter invented in their youth, and retold so often that they had come to believe in it themselves.

Nevertheless, according to the anthropologist, C. F. Haimendorf: "Most Sherpas have seen Yeti at some time or other, and wall-paintings in monasteries and temples depict two types of them—one resembling a bear and one resembling a large monkey. It is generally known that there are two such types, and in hard winters they come into the valleys and prey on the Sherpas' potato stores, or even on cattle." Shortly after my departure from the Himalayas it was reported from Kathmandu that a female yak-herder in the Everest region had been knocked unconscious by a *Yeti*, which then killed five of her animals by twisting their horns.

There are said to be two main types of *Yeti*—a small variety that feeds on humans and a large variety that prefers yaks. J. A. McNeely, an American zoologist, who was still in Nepal looking for *Yeti* at the time of my visit, has published a detailed description of the smaller variety by combining all the eyewitness accounts available. "It is a stocky ape-like creature about 5 to $5\frac{1}{2}$ feet tall, covered with short coarse hair, reddish brown or greyish brown in colour, and longer on the shoulders.

The large head has a high-pointed crown and a marked sagittal crest. Small ears lie close to the head and the face is hairless and rather flat. The teeth are quite large, though not fangs, and the mouth is wide. The arms are long, reaching to the knees. The Yeti normally walks on two legs, with a shuffling gait; he may drop to all fours when in a hurry or climbing over rocks. The feet are large, with two large prehensile toes and three smaller toes. There is no tail."

Professor R. N. Wojkowitz, an Austrian ethnologist who spent three years living among the peoples of Sikkim and Tibet, has also used eye-witness accounts to construct an equally vivid description of the larger variety of Yeti. It is said to be between seven and seven and a half feet tall when erect on its hind legs, with long arms and a powerful body covered with dark brown hair. It has an oval head running to a point at the top and an ape-like face. Both face and head are only sparsely covered with hair. "He fears the light of a fire," says Wojkowitz, "and in spite of his great strength is regarded by the less superstitious inhabitants of the Himalayas as a harmless creature that would attack a man only if wounded. From what native hunters say, the term 'snowman' is a mis-nomer, since firstly it is not human and secondly it does not live in the zone of snow. Its habitat is rather the impenetrable thickets of the high-est tracts of Himalayan forests. During the day it sleeps in its lair, which it does not leave until nightfall. Then its approach may be recognized by the cracking of branches and its peculiar whistling call.... Why does the creature undertake what must certainly be extremely wearisome expedi-tions into the inhospitable regions of snow? The natives have what sounds a very credible explanation: they say the Snowman likes a saline moss which it finds on the rocks of the moraine fields. While searching for this moss it leaves its characteristic tracks on the snowfields. When it has satisfied its hunger for salt it returns to the forest."

It is easy, of course, to dismiss such observations as superstitious fantasy or wishful thinking. But there is other evidence that is more difficult to explain. The tracks of unidentified beasts have been seen and photographed several times by mountaineers from East and West. Perhaps the most impressive evidence of this kind was provided by Eric Shipton, one of the pioneers of Himalayan exploration, on the Menlung Glacier during a reconnaissance of Everest in 1951. Dr. Michael Ward, another British climber who accompanied Shipton, has described the incident. "Our height was probably between 18,000 and 19,000 feet, and we were approaching the lower part of the Menlung Glacier. Some of the tracks that we saw were well formed, and others were rather indistinct.

This 12-inch-long footprint, reproduced here life size, is the strongest evidence of the legendary Yeti or "Abominable Snowman." It was photographed on the Menlung Glacier by Eric Shipton, leader of the 1951 Everest Reconnaissance Expedition. The footprints, which matched those of no known animal, appeared to have been made by a creature weighing more than 200 pounds. According to one popular theory, the "Snowmen" may constitute a relict community of Gigantopithecus, a prehistoric anthropoid known only from a few fossilized bones and teeth.

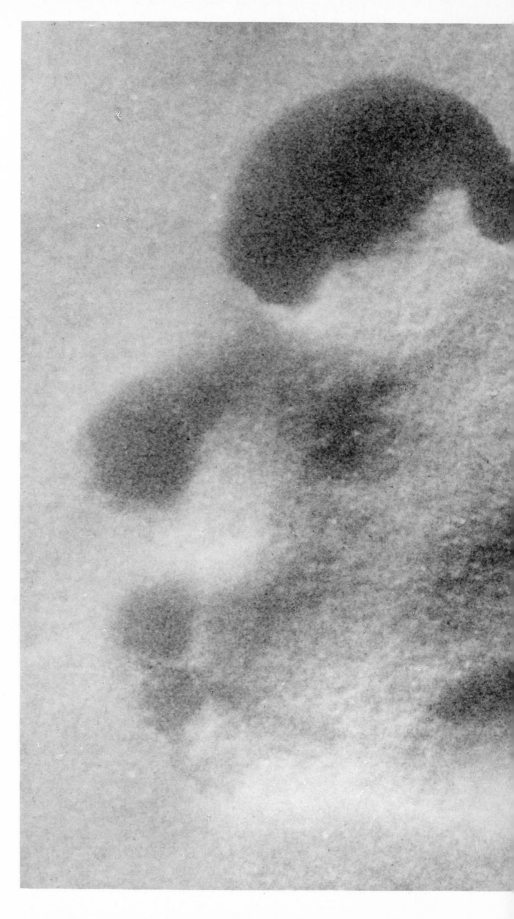

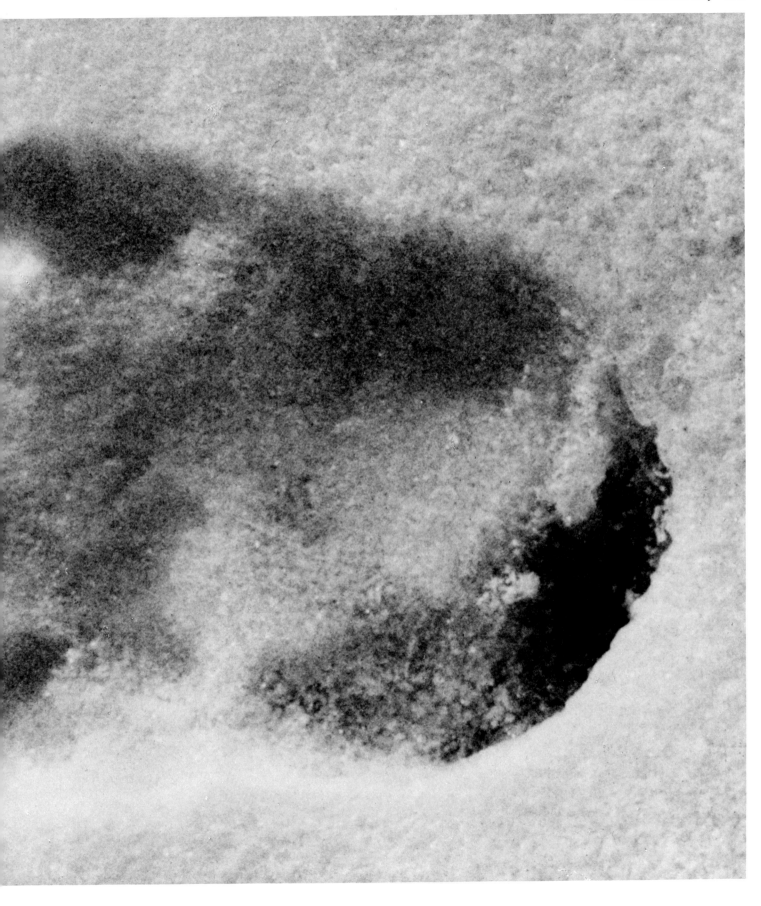

From their number it looked as though there had been more than one animal making them. They kept more or less to the middle of the glacier, and we followed the tracks for about a quarter of a mile before turning off on to a lateral moraine which led us down to some upper grassland."

From their depth the tracks had obviously been made by creatures weighing at least 200 pounds apiece. The prints were 12 to 14 inches long and about six inches wide. "The imprint that we photographed," Ward recalled, "had the impression of five definite toes. The most medial toe being the largest, as in a human foot. The small toe left very little imprint at all. The rest of the foot was very similar to that of a human being, except that, of course, it was broader. One feature was that where the animal had crossed a small crevasse one could see where the toes had dug in to gain purchase on landing, and also it appeared as though there might be the imprints of nails."

One fascinating conjecture is that *Yeti* may be related to *Giganto-pithecus*, a huge anthropoid known from the fossils of mandibles and teeth, which flourished in southern China and India about half a million years ago, when the Himalayas were still being formed and the new genus *Homo* was evolving. Driven upwards by fire-using and weapon-wielding man, *Gigantopithecus* could have taken refuge in the rising mountains and may still find sanctuary there.

But if such a creature exists, it does not appear to have survived in the western Himalayas and Karakorams, for the locals to whom I mentioned it had never heard of it. Also absent from this region are several species commonly found from Nepal to Burma. The panda, sambur, crestless porcupine and hog-badger are to be found neither in Kashmir nor farther west, and those curious goat-antelope, the grey goral and maned serow, with their short, backward-sloping horns, do not range west of Kashmir. Instead, one finds others more adapted to life in the barren mountains: the Kashmir stag (looking uncannily like its Landseer equivalent), the ibex—a goat with scimitar horns—the Marco Polo sheep and the markhor. Northwards, in the Tibetan plateau, live the wild ass, the bharal or blue sheep, the snow-leopard and the yak.

The snow-leopard, also a native of the higher Himalayas, is slightly smaller than the common leopard, with a longer tail. Its coat is soft grey to pure white, starred with pale rosettes. It rarely comes below 6,000 feet in winter, and in summer has been found in areas as high as 18,000, where it preys on the wild sheep and goats. I was always meeting people who had met other people who had seen one in the wild. Only once, in northern Pakistan, did I find an actual eye-witness. He said that the leopard was "very stupid", not reacting to danger like other wild animals. "I shot it as it stood motionless, gazing at me."

The yak is the highest-dwelling mammal in the world. Rarely, in its wild state, will it come below 14,000 feet. The domestic yak is employed in the Himalayas as low as 10,000, but when one was brought to the plains of Afghanistan, it died of liver disease within a few months. Its favoured habitat is the bleak Tibetan plateau, where it lives off wiry tufts of grass. It is the largest native animal in Tibet—a bull can weigh 1,200 pounds and stand six feet at the shoulder—and untamed is exceedingly fierce: even its tongue is so harsh that it can rasp flesh off bones. But nothing could be gentler than the domestic yaks that the Sherpas employ, moving in single file over high snowbound passes, uncanny in their power to detect hidden rocks or clefts. They are excellent riding animals. In Hunza I sat astride a yak, and found it difficult to distinguish between ascent and descent so short are its legs, so sure its gait, and so deep and soft the natural saddle of its back.

With its thick, matted coat and large lungs the yak is supremely well adapted to survive the intense cold and thin air of maximum heights. With other mammals, too, the rule is almost invariable: the higher their habitat, the larger their lungs. Birds, however, seem unaffected by the rarefied air, and expend no greater effort on sailing level with the highest peaks than low in the valleys. One Everest expedition watched lammergeyers sailing at 25,000 feet, and another was effortlessly followed by choughs—members of the crow family—to 27,000. They have no obvious reason to fly so high: there is no food for them there. Why do they do it? I put the question to Robert Fleming. He explained that high flying puts no strain upon them. They are helped by up-draughts of warm air, and can descend with equal ease whenever they wish, covering great distances very quickly. They seem to find little difficulty in breathing: a man cannot talk and breathe simultaneously at 18,000 feet, but birds twitter happily at even higher altitudes.

"So they fly high for fun?"

"Yes, for play and pleasure."

It was nice to find in the wilderness of the Himalayas a living thing that actually enjoyed it.

Denizens of the "Moist Lands"

For the eastern two-thirds of its length, the base of the Himalayas is fringed by a narrow fertile strip, 10-20 miles wide, known as the *terai*, the "moist land." Although much of it is now heavily farmed, many areas are still unchanged from the original tracts of treacherous marsh and jungle and they still provide sanctuary for a unique cross-section of Asia's wildlife.

The *terai* owes its fertile extravagance to two factors besides its rich soil: heat and water. Lying far inland at an altitude of less than 600 feet, it receives few cooling breezes, and summer temperatures exceed 100°F. Abundant water is supplied by seepage from the monsoon rains that soak the mountains at the height of summer.

After running down the foothills, the rain-water disappears into the loose gravel and rubble at their base to filter downwards at depths accessible to the roots of the trees that form the *terai*'s northern protective screen. After a gradual drop of around a thousand feet, the water seeps through to the surface when the ground levels off. Consequently, the untamed areas of the *terai* are almost impenetrable complexes of muddy, wandering streams, thick, low bush, and dim, tall forest. Nepal's Chitwan National Park, where these pictures were taken, is one such area.

Chitwan is a wildlife haven. Here roams a tenth of the world's tiger population: more than 200 of these great cats pad along the game trails in the evening and wait silently amid dense reed beds for deer and wild pig. Chitwan also provides lush pastures for 200 of the world's estimated 800 Indian rhinos, foraging through twelve-foot cuckoo grass like antique ironclad ships ploughing through heavy seas.

The *terai*'s two species of monkey exploit it in different ways. The stocky rhesus swings through its tree canopy, seeking fruit and grubs, while the long-limbed langur combs the ground for the best of root, seed and shoot. Both types are raucous and can be detected even at night by occasional bursts of screeching—perhaps a warning at the sight of a passing leopard. In the creeks and rivers lurk crocodiles, some of them fish-eaters, others lying in ambush for land-dwelling animals like the dappled deer that wander along the water's margin, almost invisible against the leaves and filtering sunlight.

In a northward view over the river Reu in Chitwan National Park, the principal animal habitats of the damp region known as the terai emerge from morning mist. Tall rushes, sedges and grass in the foreground flank the muddy waters of the Reu. The dense, marshy thickets across the river lie half-hidden by mist. Behind them thick sal-tree jungle hedges the terai. The Siwalik foothills rise into the background haze.

A group of chital deer (above) pauses on
the alert at the forest edge. Content to
graze pasture or browse among the trees,
they are at home in both marsh and
jungle. Although their spotted
camouflage is least effective against the
background of rivers, they take to the
water if pursued, and can swim well.

A langur mother and young (right),
away from their tree sanctuary and
hence doubly alert, interrupt suckling
to identify a disturbance. Although
more vulnerable when they descend,
langurs spend most of their day on the
ground, tempted down by succulent
young growth on the forest floor.

Alert for a trace of game, a tiger pauses in its patrol of terai animal trails—a daily journey that will cover several miles of jungle, marsh and riverside. Since its nose is not keen enough for tracking, the tiger stalks by sound, and its eyes pick out quarry from thick cover only on the final approach at quite short range.

Nearly submerged in its favourite bathing pool, an Indian rhinoceros escapes the heat and the myriad flies of midday. Jungle mynah birds perch on the island of its massive back, attracted by both the rhino's parasites and by insects stirred up during the great animal's wallowings.

At cooler times of the day, the rhino grazes, shoulder-deep in tall cuckoo-grass (right). Mynah birds—well known as brilliant mimics—continue in permanent attendance, feeding on the grass- and ground-dwelling insects that are scattered by the trampling progress of their six-foot high, two-ton benefactor.

A gharial (or gavial) crocodile cleaves
the water with its thin, club-like snout
as it maintains position against the
current. The snout, armed with even,
needle-like teeth, is an adaptation to the
gharial's diet of fish: it offers little
resistance to the water when the
crocodile strikes with an abrupt
sideways slash of the head. Though
fearsome to behold—the gharial can
grow to 20 feet long—this reptile is of
little danger to humans; if approached,
it simply sinks into the water.

4/ To the Edge of the World

The Karakorams are one of the highest mountain barriers in the world, where a mile can be swallowed up by a single curve of river or mountain-flank. Extending for some 300 miles from the Afghan border to the Shyok River, they divide Pakistan from China and run parallel to the Punjab Himalayas, separated from them only by the Indus Valley. Created by immense forces over astronomic periods of time, the environment is so vast, so exuberant, so menacing, that it is beyond human capacity to comprehend or constrain. Here rock and water are in perpetual but unequal competition, for rock must always yield eventually to water, shouldering it aside in one place only to admit its passage in another.

Looking south to Nanga Parbat, I saw how that huge mass delays and diverts but cannot prevent the incision of the Indus on its impetuous course to the Arabian Sea. I was standing at the confluence of the Indus with one of the major tributaries of its upper valley, the Gilgit. Each river arrives at this point apparently equal in width and vigour. But when they merge there can be no question which is master, for the Indus accepts the Gilgit in a flurry of bubbles and broken eddies that are smoothed away a quarter of a mile downstream, and then flows onwards as if nothing special had happened. That the two rivers have reached this same point at the same level is a fact of geography that one takes for granted, since it is bound to occur somewhere. But their headstreams lie 1,000 miles apart, and in hustling to their junction each drops 13,000 feet and forces its way through the mighty Karakorams.

It is possible to drive from the base of Rakaposhi in the Karakorams to the base of Nanga Parbat in the Himalayas in half a day, and as you cross the Indus by a quivering bridge of planks suspended from high wires, it seems less a frontier than a jugular vein. The Indus, like the Brahmaputra, rises in Tibet from the slopes of the superbly symmetrical Mount Kailas, sacred to Buddhist and Hindu alike.

The two rivers to which Kailas gives birth are the greatest in the Himalayas, greater than either the Irrawaddy or the Ganges, which also spring from the mountains. The Brahmaputra and the Indus are the same length—1,800 miles—and both flow parallel to the Himalayan range before breaking through it at opposite ends. The Brahmaputra receives a lot of rainfall; the Indus flows for the first part of its length in the Karakoram-Himalaya trough, which is seldom visited by rain, but is fed by melt-water, and then receives tributaries in such abundance that it carries at its mouth twice the volume of the Nile.

Such rivers make geography intelligible. They have a sense of purpose and destination; mountains have none. They are alive; mountains are inert, like the Bilcher, which presides over the Indus-Gilgit confluence. The green-blue water was the only movement in the scene before me, and added the only colour to mountain-brown and summit-white. The land is semi-desert, the water slipping past in chasms too deep to rise and irrigate the shoulder levels, where the cauldron heat of summer completes the desiccation begun by sheep and goats. The steppes are tufted by camel-thorn and sagebrush, but are otherwise barren, and the course of minor tributaries is indicated in winter only by fernlike patterns in the dust. So empty is the upper valley of the Indus that the dirt road and bridge by which I travelled were the only human marks upon it, strikingly economical in their effort compared to the wastage of mountain and river in theirs. And yet I was amazed, seeing it for the first time, that the mighty Indus, which gave its name to a whole sub-continent and to a civilization that lasted a thousand years, could make so little impact upon its surroundings.

Nanga Parbat is the western sentinel not only of the Indus Valley but of the entire Himalayan range. Its name means "naked mountain," because its steely cliffs can hold no permanent snow; and to German climbers it is known as Murder Mountain from its reputation as a man-killer. From the north it cannot be described as beautiful, for beauty in a mountain demands a certain symmetry, while Nanga is ill-proportioned, rising to 26,660 feet by a series of barren shoulders, each shrugging higher than the last and culminating in the summit of curving snow.

From other directions it seems more graceful and certainly less tame, particularly to those climbing it. I understood something of their hardships when I flew from Rawalpindi to Gilgit at 18,000 feet past its western flanks. This must be the most dramatic of all scheduled flights, but so dependent upon weather that the pilot turned back in mid-air on our first three attempts. As I was sitting next to him, I felt more grateful than frustrated. Clouds rose ahead of us larger than the mountains. We could not fly over them because the ceiling of the little Fokker aeroplane is only 20,000 feet; and we could not fly through them because Nanga might lurk like a tiger inside. Our fourth attempt succeeded, and we climbed from the plain to cross ridges that soon gathered into quills slanting steeply to minor peaks, with streams running between them like spilled ink. Against their sides stood banks of pine, no longer green from this height, but tiny black exclamation marks.

For the mountaineers this is merely the approach march, lasting weeks. Then their real difficulties begin. I looked down, then across, then upwards, at Nanga Parbat as it rose above us, and chose the routes by which I imagined myself overcoming ice-walls and crevasses, just as a huntsman can follow a scent cross-country from the windows of a train. The summit was domed and smooth and seemed easy to me. Then I remembered Hermann Buhl of Innsbruck, who in 1953 climbed the last 4,400 feet alone, leaving his companion in the highest camp at 2.30 a.m. and took until 7 that evening to reach the top, too late to descend. He spent the night under a crescent moon a few hundred feet below the summit, without oxygen, food or tent and somehow survived. When his friends went up next day to retrieve his corpse, they met him stumbling down.

Having finally landed at Gilgit, I wanted to see Nanga Parbat from closer to, and so I followed the track that climbs eventually up the eastern side of the mountain near the village of Astor. This track will take only the toughest of vehicles and it is impossible to drive from Gilgit to Astor—a distance of 70 miles—in less than five or six hours. The slowness of the journey is an indication of its hazards. For the first 40 miles, until well beyond the Indus bridge and the solitary village of Bunji, the road was rough but fairly level. It was only when our Jeep swayed over the bridge at the foot of the Astor Gorge that I began to wonder whether I should have come at all.

Here a Jeep must behave like a goat. The track is scarcely wider than the Jeep itself, and is cut from the cliff-face in a ledge that sometimes runs at river-level, but more often four or five hundred feet above it. It is slippery with ice or dust (how odd to see the two in juxtaposition), and there is no parapet of any kind on the river side to guard against the precipitous drop. As the track winds steeply upwards to hug the mountainside and gain height, there are frequent hairpin bends that the driver must approach at speed to gain the necessary impetus to round them, and these are the most alarming moments of the 30-mile ascent. He hurtles into apparently empty space, and at the last second wrenches the wheels around the corner, hoping that they will grip the ice and that there will not be a herd of goats on the other side. Then there are bends so tight that they can be turned only by reversing to the very edge of the abyss. And if you should meet a descending vehicle, which on my journey happened only once, the impasse must be overcome by retreating backwards to a strip of slightly wider path where one vehicle can squeeze past the other hub to hub, the outer wheels scraping the rock wall or manoeuvring to within an inch of oblivion. I did not want to ask how many fatal accidents there had been and, tactfully, I was not told. Still, we made it safely: up, and then down again.

Actually Nanga Parbat became less visible the nearer I approached it; and was completely out of sight once I was on its slopes. We were obliged to drive up another 2,000 feet to Ramah before the mountain began to reveal itself again, and at 13,000 I was still less than halfway up.

Ramah is a delectable place. It is not a village, but a single hut, built by British officers in the 1930s for rest and recreation. I was the first foreigner to come there in winter for five years, said the caretaker of the rest-hut. The last was another Englishman. "He had a lady with him," the caretaker added disapprovingly. The hut lies at one end of a valley that has been carved into the rock by a minor glacier. In summer it is a meadow grazed by yaks and spangled with flowers; in January it is snow-filled from end to end. Streams feed into it, flowing fast under translucent hoods of ice or past waterfalls frozen solid into glacial pillars. It is ringed by trees, mostly *Pinus wallichiana* and the edible pine, *Pinus gerardiana*, which stand ruddy in the sunlight against the snow. At the far end, two miles from the hut, is a lake in which are reflected snowpeaks 20,000 feet high. I first mistook the highest of them for Nanga Parbat itself, but the summit still lies hidden many miles beyond, and you can see it only by climbing another thousand feet up a steep spur (which the lady refused to do, said the caretaker with a sniff). On these slopes are found ibex and musk-deer, he told me. And he had often come across prints of snow-leopards.

I felt myself embraced by the Himalayas in a way I never felt at Everest or in the Gandaki Valley, for my feet were treading untrodden snow, and here at last was the stillness found only in high mountains far from human habitation. As the steel tip of my walking-stick punctured the surface ice, I imagined it an alpenstock and felt the upward tug to which all mountaineers succumb. I began to understand how they can risk their lives for the purity of it all, the purity of old rock and new snow, of the crystalline air, the cleanliness of the very danger to which they are exposed, for there could be nothing mean about death in such a place: terrible, perhaps, but never squalid.

On the return journey I stopped at Astor. It is called by its inhabitants "the city", in the sense, I suppose, of the ancient Greek concept of a city, for although it is nothing but a huddle of mean houses, it has a tradition of bellicose independence, and is now the main frontier village between Pakistan and Indian Kashmir. It is little known except to its inhabitants, who imagine it to be world-renowned as a trade route and battleground. They live a life of excruciating hardship, although it would be a simple matter to tap the great Indus River in the valley at their feet and flood and fertilize the barren plains. The streams flowing off the mountains could also be trapped and split into life-giving rivulets. My companions expressed agreement. "Come," they said. "Come to Hunza, and we will show you where it has been done."

The Hunza River splits the Karakorams from north to south, rising on the Chinese border and flowing into the Gilgit River, which, in turn, flows into the Indus. Enclosed by mountains rising to 25,000 feet, its floor cultivated like a garden, the Hunza Valley deserves Eric Shipton's encomium as "the ultimate manifestation of mountain grandeur". Poplars, thin and pale as wands in their winter nakedness, ride dead-still up the slopes or curve in groves along the river-banks. Between them are terraced orchards of apricots, apples and almonds, some interwoven with vines, and irrigated by rivulets of the clearest water falling in tresses from the nearer hills. At one point a gorge gapes at its summit to disclose the white triangle of a glacier and near by rises the tremendous granite needle known as Princess Bubula's Peak; opposite, growing misty with distance, is the glen that forms the bed of the Hispar Glacier; and at the southernmost end of the valley towers Rakaposhi, a queen of a mountain, with pink clouds streaming at sunset from a summit ridge that thrusts into the sky like a blade of steel.

One can drive the entire length of the Hunza Valley by Jeep, and for me the excitement of the journey was not so much the fabled central

A snow-leopard lazes outside its lair; sadly, the species is becoming scarce because its superb coat is highly prized by fur hunters.

section where the Hunza people live, but the gorge itself and the almost uninhabited country at its northern end. The dirt road we followed is cut much more boldly in the face of the cliff than the track to Astor. It follows grander curves, affording dizzy views downwards of the torrent swirling past rock-precipices, and upwards to sudden glimpses of mountains that appear to belong to another world. The Hunza River has literally torn the Karakorams apart. But as the process was so gradual, it has left, instead of the jagged edges found in the Astor Gorge, smooth canyon walls striped at intervals by horizontal strata of a different colour. So deep is the gorge that it receives little light direct from the sun, but the honey-coloured cliffs fill the basin with a warm glow, and we never felt claustrophobically enclosed. Turning a final bend, we saw in front of us the entrance porch to the canyon, a 10,000-foot wall of rock, pierced by the river, and crenellated by a row of sharp peaks very close together and almost equal in height. As they caught the setting sun, each one became a Gothic flambeau.

This was the route, I suddenly remembered, by which Peter Fleming in 1935 had descended to India after his six-month, 3,500-mile journey overland from Peking. On my return to England I re-read his *News from Tartary* and was amused to find with what relief he had greeted this grim scene as the first outpost of civilization. To him it had powerfully suggested Scotland. To me it was the end of the known world. In his day there was nothing but a mule-track cut in the cliff, but today the road, barely passable from Gilgit, becomes unbelievably good about eight miles beyond Baltit, the capital of Hunza. The dirt road and swaying suspension bridges give place to a three-lane highway with stone bridges, curves and gradients as smooth as a glacier's, and a surface incomparably better. It was built by the Chinese as a peace-offering to Pakistan, and parts of it are labelled with appropriate titles: Friendship Bridge; Chou En-Lai Pass. The road is still bordered by immense mountains, high enough—and thus important enough—to be named and measured. Several of them are over 25,000 feet high. From their northern slopes descend glaciers 20 or 30 miles long, two of them extending to within a quarter of a mile of the road. It is very cold—the valley lies in the middle of a natural refrigerator—and in the evening the wind from the south howls through the canyon towards Pasu.

Just beyond Pasu we were halted by a barrier across the road. It was not the Chinese frontier, which lies several miles ahead, but a Pakistani checkpoint where we were informed with courtesy and many jokes that we could go no farther. It was disappointing, but the soldiers

Throwing up clouds of sand and dust, a wave of broken rock rolls down the scree slopes of a barren valley in Hunza province.

allowed us to walk across the bed of the Hunza—mainly dry at this time of the year—to inspect its confluence with the Shimshal and sent a guide to show us the way across the half-mile of stone and ice.

Lord, this is a dreadful place. I began to understand why our ancestors pictured Hell as cold. On a summer's day, perhaps, the deep valley could acquire grandeur and even charm. But this was mid-January and night was falling. The wind increased in force and bitterness, veering from point to point in violent gusts, and all around us the cliffs turned menacing and sullen-yellow. The two great glaciers ended in dirty snouts faintly visible in the gloom, and other ice-falls were clamped to chutes of fallen rock. Mist canopied the valley. There were no birds, no trees, no plants, no animals and no people except the soldiers in their unenviable outpost. Ahead of us, as we picked a path between ice-coated boulders, we could hear the increasing roar of the Hunza River, and when we reached it, we saw the Shimshal, which rises 100 miles away to the east, forcing its way through the opposite cliff. This was no confluence; it was an ejaculation. The anger of the Hunza was simply doubled. It poured away into the mounting darkness, marking its passage by irritable white flares. As we turned back across the stones, the sky surrendered the last of the day's light, and all that remained to guide us were vast shapes blacker than the blackness that surrounded them.

Northwards from Pasu the valley opens out into a wide basin to collect the water of a large area, and we had a glimpse of it before walking to the Hunza. It seemed suddenly familiar, then I realized that I was remembering photographs of the moon. There was the same dusty plain split by bare mountains and ravines, the same motionless boulders strewn across it, the same flat light. For the most part it is empty wilderness, and at its centre, within 50 miles of where we stood, three frontiers converge, those of the Soviet Union, China and Afghanistan, while a fourth, Pakistan's, lies near by. The neighbouring places of their junctions are clearly marked on the map; on the ground they are minor peaks, and have been visited only by the most intrepid travellers. The mountains are fleshless bones that will look little different half a million years hence. No boundary fences are possible or required, and though their assumed courses have been formalized by treaty and toasted by foreign ministers in glasses of champagne, the frontiers merge in a desolate no-man's-land where all the winds of Asia meet to howl a common dirge.

Apart from a few favoured valleys like Hunza, the Karakorams are inhospitable to man, and the poverty of the people and the great distances between settlements are proof of it. Linked to the rest of Pakistan only in the last 25 years by an unreliable air service and a single Jeep track, the region has tended to look northwards towards China for its material and spiritual sustenance, rather than south to India. The carved woodwork of the Mir (Rajah) of Hunza's ancient palace at Baltit, purely Chinese in character, is one example of this. Attitudes are changing, however, as communications improve and more visitors come to Hunza.

But while Gilgit and Hunza are already feeling the effect, the eastern end of the Karakoram range, where the greatest mountains rise, is scarcely more penetrable than in 1887, when Francis Younghusband became the first European to attempt a crossing at its most perilous point. His story is worth retelling as an example of earlier explorations of this wilderness. Younghusband was a captain in the King's Dragoon Guards. Stationed in China, he determined to walk from Peking to India across the Gobi Desert and the Karakorams, a journey of 3,000 miles never previously attempted.

The first stage went well: with eight camels, a guide, a servant and a Mongol assistant, he plodded 1,000 miles through the interminable desert, mostly at night, before he came to the first house he had seen since starting. From there it was another 40 days' march to Kashgar in Chinese Turkestan, and thence south to Yarkand, where he had his first view of the mountains. He had the choice between the easier Karakoram Pass, leading to Leh, in Ladakh, or the much higher and virtually unexplored Mustagh Pass into Kashmir. He chose the latter. His guide, Wali, who had crossed this pass 30 years before—from the opposite direction—was the last man known to have done so. There were seven other men with them, and 13 ponies to carry their supplies.

But Wali, it transpired, had forgotten the way. As they entered the mountain belt, they were in pathless country untenanted by man; and on reaching the top of a 15,000-foot pass, the first, they saw ahead of them tiers of peaks—25,000, 26,000 and, in one case, 28,000 feet high. "It was a scene," wrote Younghusband, "which, as I viewed it, and realized that this seemingly impregnable array must be pierced and overcome, seemed to put the iron into my soul." They descended a steep valley, then climbed again to another pass, "where I chanced to look upwards rather suddenly, and a sight met my eyes which fairly staggered me. We had just turned a corner which brought into view a peak of appalling height, which could be no other than K2. Viewed from this direction, it seemed to rise in an almost perfect cone, but to an inconceivable height. We were quite close under it, and here on the northern side, where it is literally clothed in glacier, there must have been 14,000 to 16,000 feet of solid ice."

They advanced to the foot of the pass and found their way along a glacier composed of blocks of ice 200 feet tall. Incredibly, they led the ponies through it, hauling and pushing, slipping and falling, for 15 miles, taking advantage of whatever moraine they could find at the edges. From that point the ponies could go no farther, and leaving them with a couple of men to lead them by the alternative route, Younghusband and the six others started to climb the final pass. For equipment they had only one bedroll, a sheepskin coat for each man, some native biscuits, a large kettle, a packet of tea, an ordinary pick-axe and a bottle of brandy that Younghusband had brought all the way from Peking, promising himself not to open it until he reached India.

The ascent of the Mustagh Pass was breathless but not too hard, and they reached the top (19,030 feet) at midday. On the far side they looked down an ice-slope as steep as a house roof terminating in a precipice several thousand feet high. "To get down," wrote Younghusband, "seemed to me an impossibility. I had had no experience of Alpine climbing, and had no ice-axe or other mountain appliances. I had not even any proper boots. All I had for footgear were some native boots of soft leather without nails and without heels . . . which gave me no sort of grip on an icy surface . . . I kept quite silent as I looked over the pass, and waited to hear what the men had to say about it. They meanwhile were looking at me, and imagining that an Englishman never went back from an enterprise he had once started, took it as a matter of course that as I gave no order to go back, I meant to go on."

So they started down the ice-slope, Wali cutting steps with the pick-axe, the others following him holding a rope of which one end was tied round Wali's waist. But they did not have the sense to loop it round their own. Younghusband tied handkerchiefs round his boots to give them extra grip, and they advanced to the edge of the precipice. At that point one man turned back unable to face it. But Younghusband and the five others began their descent, taking advantage of slight holds that the rugged surface of the rock presented: "Even then we seldom got a hold for a whole hand or a whole foot. All we generally found was a little ledge, upon which we could grip with the tips of the fingers or side of the foot . . . For six hours we descended the precipice, partly rock and partly ice slope, and when I reached the bottom and looked back, it seemed impossible that any man could have come down such a place."

As the sun set, they reached the head of the Baltoro Glacier and made camp. The only casualty of the descent was the bottle of brandy, smashed in a fall. It took the party two more days to traverse the glacier, and a further two to reach Ashkole, the first inhabited spot in India—"a repulsively dirty place" where the inhabitants were most inhospitable, dismayed to find that their village was approachable from the north. Younghusband and his party continued to Skardu in Baltistan and then walked on to Srinagar. There the political agent, the first fellow-countryman he had seen for seven months, greeted Younghusband with the words, "Don't you think you should have a wash?"

Mountains and remote villages do not change much in 90 years, and Ashkole still lies three days' journey from Skardu, for the Jeep-track extends only part of the way up the Shigar Valley which leads to it, and the path is rough and steep. Shigar is not unlike Hunza. Fertile with almond trees and even grapes and tobacco, it is fed by several glaciers of which the Baltoro is one of the longest in the world outside the Polar regions. In Ashkole itself you will still find the huddle of squalid houses that represented to Younghusband the fingertips of civilization reaching out to guide him home.

This region of Baltistan contains a larger number of clustered peaks over 24,000 feet than any other area, even in the Himalayas. Sixty of them are over 22,000. The highest, K2 (28,250), is exceeded only by Everest, and the three Gasherbrums are all over 26,000. They are infinitely remote. The base of K2 lies 100 miles from the nearest point approachable on wheels, and an expedition can take three weeks to reach it before the serious climbing begins. I saw only the approaches, but enough to realize the hardship of the full journey and the dangers of the climb. The Karakorams rather than the Pamirs, to which the title is usually applied, are the Roof of the World.

The Mountain Fliers

The Himalayan slopes are home to a cosmopolitan population of birds, most of them immigrants that have colonized this apparently hostile world. They represent species from as far as Europe and Africa and as close as the neighbouring uplands of the Orient. And their life-styles reflect a vast range of habitats—from the frozen, wind-torn snow-fields of the world's highest peaks to the hot and forested foothills.

The highest realm belongs to the birds of prey and carrion. The perils of life near the snow-line ensure a constant supply of carcases: predators leave the remains of their kills and any mountain sheep or goat that weakens soon succumbs to cold. This food supply attracts huge griffon vultures. Their ominous shadows are as familiar on the Himalayan snows as are those of their counterparts on the African plains, and they spiral on wind currents up to 25,000 feet. Their more ornate cousins, the lammergeyers, now almost extinct in their European homeland, also skim the high contours, and alpine choughs—members of the crow family—have been seen as high as 27,000 feet.

On and below the snow-line at 9-15,000 feet, where melting snow provides water for the alpine pastures and attendant insects, lies an area rich in food for the smaller birds. This is the summer home of many species; redstarts and accentors, sparrow-sized insect-hunters, flit from boulder to boulder or dash, mouse-like, in pursuit of their minute prey. Pheasants, partridges and pigeons from the heights of China feed on shoots and bulbs; their colours blend with the patchwork of grass, boulders and snow, helping them avoid the attention of eagles and hawks.

Many of the snow-line birds are seasonal commuters. Nesting at summer-time in the safety of the snows, they fly down to the forests of the foothills, as low as 5,000 feet in winter. There they must adopt an entirely different style of life. Although food and shelter are readily available, competition is fierce, for the lower jungles and forests teem with birds: green parakeets scream from the treetops, flocks of strutting mynahs flit restlessly from clearing to clearing, and undulating files of thrush-like brown babblers flop heavily from bush to bush, seeking seeds. It is a world rich in food, and vastly different from the austere and lonely heights.

As pre-monsoon clouds swirl around the snow-line, griffon vultures wheel effortlessly. With wings that can span 10 feet, griffons are masters of gliding, so the savage updraughts caused by drastic temperature changes and towering rockfaces enable them to cover great distances in quest of food.

This rare picture of a lammergeyer on the ground—it is resting on the stony fringes of an alpine pasture—reveals the rich tawny colour of the bird's breast, which is so difficult to see when the bird is flying against a bright sky. Also visible is the moustache of black feathers that gives the lammergeyer its other name of bearded vulture.

In flight, the lammergeyer specializes in fast, contour-hugging glides. It can reach 80 m.p.h. in its sweeping searches for skeletons picked clean by its cousins, the griffon vultures. When successful, it seizes a large bone in its talons, flies high over rocks, drops its burden to shatter it and then lands to make a meal of the marrow.

Blood pheasants forage for pine shoots, mosses, ferns and lichen in the world's highest pheasant habitat: the melting snow at 9-15,000 feet. In contrast to the eye-catching plumage of the males (centre)—their stripes account for the "blood" of their name—the females (far right) are a dowdy brown. Their dull colour provides camouflage when they incubate their eggs in grass-lined gaps between boulders.

An insect-hunter of the upper slopes, the alpine accentor (left) scours crevices for flies and beetles. Winter drives it down to the forest, where it must compete for food, but the accentor, with a muscular throat that can break up hard seeds, is adapted to the change.

Snow pigeons (right) glide the last few hundred feet to feeding grounds in the cliffs and forests at around 9,000 feet. They make this downhill journey once a day, flying back up before dusk, no matter what the weather, to roost in valleys above the snow-line, where they gather to be secure from predators.

Alert to every movement in the tangled undergrowth, a spiny babbler sits on its nest in the low scrubland of Nepal. Among the shyest of hill-side birds and a weak flier, it keeps to the low bushes in its search for insects. Although occasionally tempted from cover to feed in near by grasslands, the spiny babbler seldom ventures into regions that are above 6,000 feet.

5/ The Great Divide

The general impression of the great range is of a wild, desolate, little-known country, a country of great peaks and deep valleys, of precipitous gorges and rushing grey-green rivers; a barren beautiful country of intense sunlight, clear sparkling air and wonderful colouring.

W. K. FRASER-TYTLER/ *AFGHANISTAN*

Before I left London I rang up the Afghan Embassy.

"Please, I want a visa for Afghanistan."

"Why exactly?"

"Because I am writing a book about the Himalayas."

"We have no Himalayas in Afghanistan."

The voice at the other end sounded like a high-class florist from whom I had ordered two dozen saucepans.

"Yes, you have: the Hindu Kush."

"The Hindu Kush are not part of the Himalayas."

"They are as much part of them as a bridal train is part of a wedding-dress."

This was too elaborate an argument to sustain over the telephone with a complete stranger, and the voice repeated, more emphatically, its earlier denial, and rang off.

Later, when I went to the Embassy in person, they were just as sceptical, but put it more kindly.

"The Hindu Kush are hardly the Himalayas themselves. Are you quite sure that you wish to include them?"

I was quite sure. Geographically they are *extensions* of the Himalayas, I said, and if we left them out we would make ourselves look ridiculous.

I got my visa with no trouble at all, indeed with great courtesy, and being committed, went to see the Hindu Kush. There is no difficulty in *seeing* them: you have only to look out of a hotel window in Kabul, the Afghan capital. They smash across the horizon like great towers. To *visit* them, in mid-winter, when I was there, is a different matter. The range is 600 miles long, rising to 25,000 feet, and is crossed by three roads that lead northwards from Kabul to the Russian frontier. Only one, however, remains motorable throughout the year. Elsewhere, the range is impenetrable, except on foot and with great endurance. Even the hardy nomads who live deep within the hills are driven to seek shelter in the valleys. Having chosen to arrive in February, I crawled up the lower slopes of the range, hammered at its portals, flew over it, and once crossed it by car. I fought the Hindu Kush, but did not fight it very hard, and cannot claim to know it. I simply came to realize that there was more to know than any human being could compass in a lifetime.

The name Hindu Kush means "Hindu killer", and it first appears in a book of travels by the Arabian, Ibn Batuta, in 1334, in which he explains: "Many of the slaves, male and female, brought from India, die on the passage of this mountain owing to the severe cold and quantity of snow." The Greeks called it Parapamisus, derived from the Persian *uparisena*—"the peaks over which the eagle cannot fly". It is a sprawling range, with a well-defined crest-line, but serrated by deep gorges and throwing off subsidiary ridges north and south—"a barren beautiful country of intense sunlight," wrote W. K. Fraser-Tytler, the former British Minister in Afghanistan, in his classic book, *Afghanistan*, "clear sparkling air and wonderful colouring as the shadows lengthen and the peaks and rocks above turn gold and pink and mauve in the light of the setting sun".

The range curves across Afghanistan like a giant backbone, dividing the country into two unequal parts. About a third lies north of this watershed. There the peaks gradually give way to high plateaux and the plains beside the low Amu Darya (as the Oxus River is now known). Southwards from the main massif, rocky tendrils stretch in all directions, split by a series of ice-fed rivers, until they peter out in the desert flats of Iran and the plains of Kandahar. In the east the Hindu Kush narrows to the Wakhan Corridor, a spur of Afghanistan that was deliberately created in the late 19th Century to separate Russia from northern India at a time when international tensions were too great to risk a common frontier.

It is a region that few travellers have visited, and those who have find themselves overwhelmed by the violence of the terrain. "It is a country of extremes," wrote Fraser-Tytler, "of high barren plateaux and wide open stretches of sun-baked desert, of narrow fertile valleys, and rocky mountain spurs. Its climate varies from the bitter cold of the Kabul winter when the temperature frequently drops below zero Fahrenheit, to the great heat of the Oxus Valley where in summer a temperature of 110°F. is normal. It is a treeless windswept country, where in winter an icy blast blows off the high ridges, and in summer whirling 'devils' of sand and dust sweep across the open plains."

Unlike the Himalayan range itself, the Hindu Kush gets little benefit from the seasonal monsoon rains that turn the valleys of Nepal and Sikkim into lush green gardens. The average rainfall for the whole of Afghanistan is only seven inches a year, and the Hindu Kush is almost entirely bare of plants and trees except where the valleys are watered by the streams from high glaciers and winter snows. "That which most forcibly strikes a traveller in these regions," wrote Captain John Wood of his journey through the Hindu Kush in 1837-38, "is the total absence of wood—the nakedness of the country. There are no timber-yielding trees indigenous to the Hindu Kush . . . except the Arch, a dwarfish fir, which never equals in size its congeners of the Himalayan forest. It serves, however, for the building purposes of the natives, and is too valuable to be used as fuel. The poplar is seen by the sides of most rivulets, but never in great numbers, and always in localities which indicate that man has placed it there. The same may be said of fruit-bearing trees, except the almond and pistachio-nut, which are evidently natives of the lower portions of the Hindu Kush."

It is probable that there are even fewer trees in the area now than when Captain Wood was there. Droughts have increased the aridity and in 1969-70 and 1970-71 there was no winter snow at all. The immediate effect of this latest drought, however, was too much water. Without fresh falls of snow to reinforce it, the ancient snowcrust high up on the Hindu Kush began to melt, causing floods and landslip. On the southern slopes the snow-line crept upwards by as much as 1,000 feet. As well as natural disasters, the drought also brought a minor civil war. As the snow melted, new veins of semi-precious lapis lazuli were exposed and rival claims to mining rights ended in bloody fighting.

Despite this region's general aridity, however, wildlife, though scarce, is varied. There are wolves, bears, foxes, wildcats, hares, wild sheep, ibexes, porcupines, striped hyenas and the occasional leopard. Tigers have also been reported in the mountains, but evidence is scarce. Bears are present in the wooded areas of east Afghanistan and

Receiving virtually no rainfall from the monsoon, the starkly rugged heights of the Hindu Kush can only support scant vegetation.

hyenas are to be found in the south, close to the Pakistan border. The only monkeys are the rhesus, which inhabit the woods alongside the Bagshal River. Trout teem almost undisturbed in the mountain rivers, and the Amu Darya contains giant sturgeon. But the wildlife that is most visible in the mountains is the birds. The high skies are rarely clear of birds of prey, wheeling and soaring on powerful upcurrents of air. There are buzzards, eagles, occasional black kites, hawks and vultures, including lammergeyers, with their distinctive feathered necks and long wings. In the valleys snipe step cautiously through marshland and kingfishers dart over the water in a flash of bright blue.

Some of the smaller birds fall victim to the tribesmen's passion for falconry, which is evident in many of the mountain villages where men and boys can be seen with trained birds on their wrists. Hawking was probably introduced into Afghanistan by the Mongols who, in turn, are thought to have learned the sport in China where it was known as early as 2,000 B.C. Fortunately for other bird life in the Hindu Kush, a trained falcon is extremely expensive and the bird is not easy to trap. The hunter crouches in a hole in the ground and is covered with a large flat stone that has an opening in it large enough for him to put a hand through. A small bird is then tethered to the top of the stone. When the falcon drops from the sky to grab the bait, the hunter thrusts his gloved hand through the hole and grabs the predator by its talons.

I first glimpsed the eastern Hindu Kush from two valleys that ride northwards from the plain of Peshawar in Pakistan—the valleys of Swat and Chitral. I visited them both before journeying on to Kabul. The Swat is a paradise that deserves to be better known, a happy country of unique beauty and historic richness. No European had entered it for 2,000 years before British soldiers penetrated the Malakand Pass in 1895. But it was and is thickly populated, and the ruins of a hundred Buddhist monuments of an earlier age still stand as blunted cones in the corners of fields. In A.D. 519 a Chinese traveller, Sung Yun, reported that the sound of temple bells filled the whole country. Since the 16th Century it has been the home of the Yusafzai tribe, who combine a fierce disposition with remarkable skill in the arts of agriculture.

The road through Swat from Malakand is not a Jeep-track, but well-engineered tarmacadam lined with poplars. I drove up a side-valley that ended at Marghuzar below high wooded mountains, and all the way the terraced fields were green with the shoots of a very early spring. Deodar cedars dropped their ruddy needles on pale grey boulders. Aloft there were bold ridges sprouting trees and streams tumbling between euca-

Banking heavily with splayed wings, a griffon vulture strays accidentally across the flight-path of a lammergeyer that is preparing to land.

lyptus. The water is put to excellent use: first, it runs through cottages to provide a permanent tap and sink; flowing onwards, it works a water-mill; then it irrigates the upper fields; and finally—not a drop wasted—it falls in cascades to perform the same service lower down.

Quite close to Marghuzar is Udegram, the town that has been identi-fied with Ora, captured by Alexander the Great at his first assault. The present ruins are of a later fortress on the same site, and I climbed them, led by a shepherd boy. We toiled up a slope of sliding shale ridged at intervals by the foundations of houses, until, at 2,000 feet above the valley, we reached the drum-towers and ceremonial staircase of the citadel. Looking across the Swat River to the mountains on the far side, it was easy to imagine the terror inspired by the sight of Alexander's cavalry, his 30,000 infantry, his 30 elephants, flooding through the passes to the valley floor. Northwards on the horizon was the Hindu Kush, the bare hills of the middle-ground lifting suddenly into snow peaks, Falakser prominent among them at 19,500 feet. The higher and farther I gazed above the valley mist, the sharper became the outlines. The distant ice was streaked with dark shadow.

Next day I drove with a guide towards the northern wall. At first the road led along level ground on one side of the three-mile-wide valley. Then we entered the hills, and fields gave place to forest, plainsmen to highlanders. With the mountain named Mankial now presiding over the gorge, we entered the first snow. On each side of the Swat Gorge oak merged with deodar, and pine marched with gleaming needles to the frost of the river bed. Soon snow obliterated all detail of the ground, except where the trees rose thick and high and held it like a canopy over the bare rock. Eventually we reached Kalam, at 7,000 feet, where two rivers meet to form the Swat, and the driver protested that he could go no farther because the good road ends there and the Jeep-track was far too dangerous. So we walked.

We walked for three hours up the path towards Ushu and the border with Gilgit. All the way we were enclosed by the deodar forest, the cedar that can shoot up 45 feet in 20 years. Here in the northern extremity of Pakistan the tree is particularly magnificent, rising 100 feet before the first branches, marvellously symmetrical and regal. It was a Wenceslas scene: the snowtrack winding between pillar-like boles, the roar of the torrent, the high peaks beyond. In spring the ground is starred with pale-blue violets, but I was glad to see it in its winter dress. The thin mountain air awakes all one's senses: smells are sharper, sounds echo, eyesight is keener. The trodden snow is springy and aching limbs seem suddenly to be suffused with new energy at these exciting altitudes.

Chitral, the neighbouring valley, is much more difficult of access than Swat. The rough road is open for only three months in the year, and the best approach is by air from Peshawar. The journey is worth its minor perils. The state is about the size of Wales, hemmed in by mountains more than 20,000 feet high. In deep valleys nature is kind and they are filled with fruit trees, but beyond, wrote Sir George Robertson of his journey in 1890, "are vast silent mountains cloaked in eternal snow, wild glacier-born torrents, cruel precipices, and pastureless hillsides where the ibex and the markhor find a precarious subsistence. It takes time for the mind to recover from the depression which the stillness and melancholy of the landscape at first compel. All colour is purged away by the sun-glare, and no birds sing."

It is very different at the other exit from the Peshawar plain, the Khyber Pass. Here the mountains descend to manageable size (the highest point of the road is only 3,500 feet), so manageable, indeed, that men have taken over the defences from nature. The very name Khyber has a cutlass ring about it. Not only has it been throughout history a main route of invasion between India and Central Asia, but it is the home of the Afridi tribe, estimated to be 200,000 strong, and possibly the most ferocious, independent and warlike race ever known. The pass is not like Malakand, a knife-edge approached by a tortuous ascent, but a tumbled mass of hills extending 50 miles from side to side, not so much a gorge as a series of ambush positions.

I drove across it from Peshawar to Kabul in an easy day. I had ordered a car. I was given a small bus. "But I don't want a bus," I protested. "I am your only passenger." The driver, an Afridi, looked at me through a slit of the garment that swaddled him from head to foot. "I have friends," he said; and I did not dare challenge the look in his eyes. So we set off, and at intervals stopped to pick up the friends, who mounted alongside me, saying nothing, gripping rifles.

At the mouth of the pass the villages and individual farms are contained within high mud walls, like minor forts, windowless but loopholed for small arms. We began to twist into the first hills by an excellent road, the railway winding above and below it, the old caravan route braided between them. A team of donkeys trotted past below us, bearing huge rubber tyres, slung like panniers one to each side. A fort or fortlet crowned each hill, and on the few faces of sheer rock were carved the crests of British regiments. It was all very reassuring. Then my driver began signalling to other friends on the road in what appeared to be a finger-code—two fingers, three, one bent double—and I imagined how sinister such signs could seem in less peaceful times. I barely noticed when we reached the summit, for the whole Khyber is less a crossing than a weaving between huge mounds. The frontier was like a Mafia headquarters, but the soldiers on each side were friendly. I entered Afghanistan with the sense of having survived an unpleasant experience, though nothing unpleasant had occurred. It is a haunted place: the tension of past history is still felt.

During the long drive onwards to Kabul the Hindu Kush kept me company on the horizon. I bought oranges and bananas in Jalalabad and shared them with my silent companions, and we drove on and on through wide plains covered with herds of goats, and then through the three long gorges of the Kabul River, very narrow and turbulent. Walled villages were flung at intervals against the lower hills, the houses catching the light or throwing strong shadows, as in a cubist painting.

From Kabul the Hindu Kush is seen in all its splendid eminence, enlarged in winter by the spreading of the snow to cover the foothills and part of the plain. The crest-line is more regular than that of the Himalayas, forming a rampart some 15,000 feet high. I was determined to cross it. I headed across the plain of Koh-i-Daman, leaving on the right the site of Kapisa where Alexander probably wintered his troops before attempting the ascent, and on the left the village of Istalif, which was loved by Babur, the first Mogul emperor of India. Camels stalked beside the road. There were big mulberries everywhere and well-tended vines, and many of the houses had drying-floors for the grapes, lined with holes like a columbarium for the warm air to blow through.

The road leads to the Salang Pass and leaps from the plain like a thrown coil. From this point it is Russian-built, and as it mounts higher its engineering grows more extravagant, carried on vast embankments and protected from the snow by concrete galleries, until, at 11,000 feet, it pierces the crest by a tunnel one and half miles long, gloomy, cold, faintly lit by fluctuating electricity, like a mine. On the far side the road twists down again, littered with the wreckage of lorries. Failing brakes spell disaster on this descent. An hour before I reached the spot, a lorry had run amok and hurtled across the loop of a hairpin bend. Ploughing across a field of boulders, the chassis was stopped abruptly by one of them, leaving the cab and its load of grain to shoot onwards another 100 yards and disintegrate. All three occupants were killed.

I had intended to stay a few days on the summit of the Salang in a

Spiny tussocks of mauve Acantholimons stand firm while the hot, dry wind of the Hindu Kush buffets the silky threads of Stipa grass.

shanty village euphemistically renamed a skiing centre, but there were no skiers, and conditions were impossibly grim. It shares its electric current with the tunnel, and as the tunnel takes priority, the illumination of the huts is reduced to glow-worm insignificance in the evening, and to total darkness at 8 pm. I would have been miserable to no purpose throughout the long cold nights, and in daylight I would have had the choice between walks on the road, breathing diesel fumes, or stumbling across slopes obscured by snowfields so blinding that already I was forced to cover my eyes and peer through slatted fingers. I would have learned nothing; enjoyed nothing but the recollection of my misery. So I descended the north side of the pass to the valley at Khinjan, and there I spent five happy days exploring as much of the Hindu Kush as was accessible by long walks.

The Hindu Kush is a Great Divide, and its crest, as jagged as a cock's, as arrogant as Guelph architecture, was penetrable only in summer before the Russians built the all-seasons road. The passes are true passes, not clefts, and the history of Afghanistan is dominated by attempts to cross them. Alexander in 328 B.C. and Timur (Tamerlane) in A.D. 1398, used the Khaiwak Pass (11,640 feet); Babur in 1504 crossed by the Qipchak Pass (13,900), and Genghis Khan in 1220 took the lower route by Bamiyan. Alexander led 32,000 men over the Khaiwak in May, when snow still masked the northern tracks, and they suffered terribly, not so much from cold as hunger, for the ascent took a week, the descent ten days, and there was no edible vegetation on the route, no beasts except their own horses to kill, and they ate the flesh raw for lack of fuel to cook it on. When Timur took his Mongols across he could see no way down the far side except by ordering them to slide on their behinds. Timur himself had a wicker basket made, in which he was lowered by ropes to their full extent. Then a platform was cut in the snow, and the process repeated five times until he reached more level ground. The pack-animals were tied to wooden sledges and swung by ropes across the ravines. More men were lost in that crossing than in the whole of the subsequent campaign.

I saw something of this, in even crueller weather, from the foot of the passes, and suffered in imagination the agony of their climb. Snowfields one can cross with relative security, probing with a stick ahead; if necessary, glaciers can be traversed, as they were by Timur, on hands and knees; bare rock affords hand- and toe-holds. But smooth snow, covering a cascade of boulders, obliterating goat-paths, filling crevasses, creates the worst of all conditions, particularly when there are

Two pikas emerge from their hole under the rocks to forage for the grasses and scrub plants on which they feed. Small rodents that are particularly well adapted to survive extreme cold, they have been found living at 17,500 feet in the Himalayas—higher than any other mammal. Well insulated by their dense grey-brown fur, they also have furred soles enabling them to move over smooth rock. Instead of hibernating they live on grass that they have collected and stored near their burrows during the summer months.

no trees to mark the depth of snow and provide roots and trailing branches to climb by. At night there was no shelter from the smothering blizzard; no hot food; a man once frost-bitten was left to die; and those who survived had to endure all this for two weeks or more, and probably fight a battle when they reached the plain.

I fought no battle, except against the elements. Day after day I strode the paths radiating from Khinjan, away from the village and the road, and up the mountainside to the point where man-made tracks gave place to goat-paths, strewn with lumps of schist that sounded musically when kicked. These led me to the first thin slivers of encrusted ice. It is always a splendid moment. To feel ice beneath your boots and the sun reflected on your face by mirror-surfaces, to walk onwards with caution but also with mounting exhilaration, is to know what the earliest travellers knew, for these things do not change. I was soon lost in hanging valleys, lost but for one sure guide—that downward slopes at this medium height must always lead back to safety. But there can be accidents up here: a twisted ankle, if nothing worse, can immobilize a man, and the proximity of help a few thousand feet below is little consolation if his voice will carry no farther than a few hundred.

Once I thought I had come near to disaster. There was a conveniently placed thorn-bush above me on a low cliff, but it came away as I grasped it, and I fell backwards upon a bed of rocks. The fall was no more than a few feet, and the rocks were fortunately rounded, but I was hurt enough to convince myself momentarily that I had suffered some crippling injury. Of course, I hadn't. Because the human body is supple and cushioned, a superficial abrasion does no damage to its structure. But as I lay there, all the pleasure of the climb drained from me. The mountain had become hostile, the snow-couch on to which I eased myself seemed suddenly a mortuary slab. So small a space does a man occupy in this vastness that he is reduced in spirit by the contrast when he is in trouble, just as he is enlarged by it when he strides the moraines freely and alone.

That day I limped down, humbled. But there were other days when I rose at dawn and walked until dusk, and the world seemed to hold no greater joy than this, and no more splendid mountains than the Hindu Kush. Their summits were unattainable by me, but in miniature I could scale them by imagining each ridge and hummock to be the highest point. It is a slow business. Each footfall must be calculated ahead, every fresh advance measured against the difficulty of retreat. At various

This lake is set like a sheet of lapis lazuli deep into the rough, arid terrain of the Hazarajat range of the Hindu Kush in Afghanistan. It is one of five lakes fed by waters of the Band-i-Amir River. Lying at an altitude of 10,000 feet in a series of terrace-like levels, they are separated and surrounded by vertical cliffs. Even during the summer months their vivid blue waters are ice-cold.

points I crossed in ignorance thin bridges of snow, soft and all-smothering, a deceptive disguise for what lay beneath. There was no need for maps, for the very shape of the mountains is a sufficient guide for a day's slow journey, and no map will warn the climber of hazards that can only be measured by the eye and tested by the foot or stick.

In these high mountains winter seems the natural, the permanent, season. The descent of the snow-line by a few thousand feet merely makes it more accessible from the valleys, the summits more remote. The conditions aloft are duplicated by conditions lower down. One can share the experience of mountaineers without being one. What in summer is a cleft of rock becomes in winter a crevasse; a scree-slope turns into a temporary glacier. All life is extinguished where animals grazed three months before, and where they will graze again when spring returns. The levels merge. A snow-filled gully leads to a greave of ice that from its convex thickness seems perennial. A rocky outcrop is sheathed in white armour not unlike the mica of its summer state. The wilderness is extended downwards until it meets the foothills, and expectant nature rests and waits.

Conditions in other parts of the Hindu Kush are even sterner. The Anglo-Russian boundary commission of 1895 described the eastern end of the Wakhan Corridor in terms unusually vivid for an official report: "A rugged and inaccessible spur of the Sarikol range carries the boundary into regions of perpetual ice and snow to its junction with the main range. Here, amidst a solitary wilderness 20,000 feet above sea level, absolutely inaccessible to man and within the ken of no living creatures except the Pamir eagles, the three great Empires [of Britain, Russia and China] actually meet."

To the south-west of the Wakhan Corridor lies Nuristan. Walled in on all sides by mountains, it is impassable in the winter months. It is so isolated that until recent times the inhabitants were able to maintain their ancient pagan religion in a country peopled elsewhere entirely by Muslims. Until 1895, when the area was invaded, the central government in Kabul had no control of these deep upland valleys. The old name of Kafiristan, "country of unbelievers," was then changed to Nuristan, "country of light," to mark the forcible conversion of these wild people to the state religion.

They are quite unlike other races to be found in Afghanistan. The legend that they are descended from the stragglers of Alexander's army, which skirted the country on its way to Samarkand, sounds too fantastic to believe. But Eric Newby, the British explorer and travel writer, saw many people who had a distinctly southern European appearance. "They were all extraordinary," he wrote, "because they were all different, no two alike. They were tall and short, light-skinned and dark-skinned . . . There were men like gypsies with a lock of hair brought forward in ringlets on either side of the forehead. There were men with great bushy beards and moustaches that made them look like Arctic explorers. There were others like early Mormons with a fuzz of beard round their faces but without moustaches. . . . Those who were hatless had cropped hair and the younger ones, especially those with rudimentary beards, looked as strange and dated as the existentialists of St. Germain des Prés; while those whose beards were still in embryo were as contemporary as the clients of a *Café Espresso*."

From Kabul I flew to Teheran. Rising from the snow-scraped airport, I looked down upon the foothills of the Hindu Kush, white and rumpled like bedclothes. The few villages were besieged by winter; not a man-made track approached them. Above rose minor peaks untrodden since the creation. I could see clearly etched in the snow the pattern of watercourses, the gullies leading to streams, the streams to rivers, the rivers sometimes to the sea, but more often to the deserts or swamps round Kandahar, where they evaporate in temperatures as high as 115° F. It was difficult to identify places, for height, form and colour tended to merge into one, but I thought I saw the Bamiyan Valley, a slot between parallel ridges, where the Hindu Kush slowly dies away.

Above, a dark-blue sky shaded downwards to pale blue, and pale blue to misty white, soon indistinguishable from the snow with which it merged on the horizon. I followed the racing landscape through binoculars, as if equipped with magic boots. A huge plain rushed to meet us, wrinkled like leather. The pilot told us we were crossing the border of Iran. Snow again, streaked as if by monster ski-tracks, and then 1,000 miles of nothing. The Hindu Kush, and with it the whole backbone of Central Asia, had finally surrendered to the plain.

The War of the Flowers

"Plants, in a state of nature, are always warring with one another, contending for the monopoly of the soil," wrote Sir Joseph Dalton Hooker, one of the first botanists to make an extensive study of Himalayan flora in the 19th Century. "Every modification of climate, every disturbance of the soil . . . favours some species at the expense of others." Perhaps the best place to observe the effects of this struggle is the Himalayas, where the extreme height and mass of the mountains, their position between the plains of India and the highlands of Central Asia and the fact that much of the area lies in the track of the monsoon rains, provide a wide variety of growing conditions.

Although the Himalayas contain numerous habitats, they can be broken down for the sake of convenience into four broad and contrasting regions: the rain forest of the east, drenched by the monsoon and ranging up to an altitude of 6,000 feet; the wet alpine zone above the tree-line beginning at about 10,000 and rising to 18,000 feet or more; a transitional semi-wet region in the central portion of the mountains, where the precipitation from the monsoon diminishes markedly; and an arid region in the high Hindu Kush, far to the west.

In each of these regions, the plants are magnificently adapted to the exacting demands of their particular environment—some, as the pictures on the following pages demonstrate, in ingenious ways. Where living room is at a premium, as in the overgrown jungle of the lower slopes, they must compete with one another for available space and light. But the higher up the mountains or the farther west they live, the more they must engage in another, even harsher battle. Pitted against the raking winds, often covered by snow for long winter periods and oppressed by temperatures that may reach tropical intensity by summer day and plunge below zero at night, most hug the ground and may insulate themselves in a protective cocoon of fluff. Many —like the blue poppy at right—have evolved brilliant colours to lure the few available insects. A few are even qualified by evolutionary combat to survive on the wind-blasted upper slopes. One tiny plant, *Stellaria decumbens*, grows as far up as 20,130 feet, which makes it one of the highest living plants in the world, a true veteran of the war.

Considered one of the most beautiful of Himalayan plants, a species of blue poppy, Meconopsis horridula, glittering here with rain, adorns meadows and screes from 13,000 to 17,000 feet. Its forbidding Latin name is derived from the plant's armoury of straw-coloured spines which, protruding from its leafy rosettes, stems and sepals, discourage browsing animals.

LEONTOPODIUM STRACHEYI—HIMALAYAN EDELWEISS

GENTIANA DEPRESSA—HIMALAYAN TRUMPET GENTIAN

Weathering the Heights

In the alpine zone of the eastern Himalayas, flowering plants have two fundamental problems to contend with—the cold and the heavy precipitation of the monsoon.

The saussurea (right) wraps itself in a gauze of fibres that not only serve as insulation, but may prevent it from being bowed down or even undermined by torrential rain. The edelweiss (top left)—taller by several inches in the Himalayas than its cousin in the Alps—has fuzzy petals that are, in fact, protective leaves surrounding the real flowers. These are no more than tiny clusters at the centre. The leaves may also provide firm footing for pollinating insects.

The gentian's vase-shaped flowers (bottom left) dwarf the mother plant from which they spring in an effort to attract insects, but they close up tightly with the first drops of rain, a reaction that prevents them from filling up and drowning. They reopen within minutes of the sun reappearing.

SAUSSUREA TRIDACTYLA—SOW'S EAR

IMPATIENS GLANDULIFERA—HIMALAYAN BALSAM

The Space Searchers

Below the alpine zone in the eastern Himalayas lies the steamy jungle. Here on the damp slopes, different species exploit every possible niche in an intensely competitive search for space and energy-producing light.

Some are rampant climbers, with twining shoots or tendrils that clasp the trunks of evergreen oaks, sal and other trees as they reach towards the sun. *Raphidophora glauca*, whose flower is seen right, extends long aerial roots (in addition to the main root at its base) that sink into the moss of trunks soaring to 100 feet or more. Its lofty perch ensures efficient propagation: birds eat its fruits and excrete the seeds on to the ground.

The Himalayan balsam, *Impatiens glandulifera* (left) occupies an entirely different habitat. It nestles in shady gullies, tolerant of both wet and shade. When its fruit is ripe, the pod explodes, shooting seeds as much as eight feet across the forest floor to help propagation.

RAPHIDOPHORA GLAUCA FLOWER

DELPHINIUM BRUNONIANUM

Plants in the Middle

In western Nepal and the eastern Hindu Kush, where the monsoon dissipates itself, the Himalayas are a meeting place for the most adaptable species of the wetter and drier regions to the east and west.

Here large tufts of *Aster flaccidus* (right) colour the rocky mountain slopes, and the common gentian of the region is the earth-hugging *Gentiana falcata* (bottom left). *Delphinium brunonianum* (left) proliferates between 12,000 and 18,000 feet but, thwarted finally by the altitude, produces dwarf-size plants in the hard conditions at higher levels.

GENTIANA FALCATA

ASTER FLACCIDUS

Western Way of Life

In the arid Hindu Kush, in the Himalayan far west, plants can withstand long periods of drought. Many have leaves that are little more than spines, thus diminishing water loss and discouraging browsing by goats and yaks. Some produce airborne seeds that allow them to propagate themselves over a wide area: those of *Acantholimon lycopodioides* (below) are wafted away in paper-thin "shuttlecocks".

Cardamine loxostemonoides (right) also releases tiny seeds to the winds, but it has an additional means of propagation: its tiny bulbs subdivide into bulblets that roll beneath the scree to suitable environments in which to sprout.

ACANTHOLIMON LYCOPODIOIDES

CARDAMINE LOXOSTEMONOIDES

136/

6/ Man Against the Wilderness

Both man and mountain have emerged from the same original Earth and therefore have something in common between them.

SIR FRANCIS YOUNGHUSBAND/ *THE EPIC OF MOUNT EVEREST*

I sometimes tell myself an imaginary story. Long before the Europeans came to the Himalayas, a young man of the mountains looked up at the great peak that overhung his village, and without telling anyone he set out one early dawn to climb it. For days he struggled up ice and rock, hauling himself from ledge to ledge, sleeping wrapped in his cloak on perilous shelves and gnawing the frozen lump of yak's meat that he carried. On the twentieth day he reached the summit. He had climbed the highest point on earth, though he did not know it. When he came down, nobody credited that he had done what he claimed, so he gave up talking about it. But there was one person who did believe him: his son, who passed on the story to his own son, and he to his, and so on for many generations, until the Englishmen came to the village. They heard the story, and laughed. But when they, too, reached the peak of Everest, they wondered: was it possible that someone had stood there before them?

I tell myself the story only to refute it. It could not have happened. No man could reach or live at that altitude without equipment; and no Sherpa would have wished to attempt it, for the people who are forced to live permanently among the mountains look upon them with very different attitudes from those of Westerners.

In the recent past mountaineers tended to attribute to their porters romantic notions of adventure and appreciation of scenic grandeur that were unknown to the people who wrest their living from these desolate regions. The fact is that if some of them have made a profession of portering for the foreigner, this is only because it is lucrative. Most still see the peaks as holy places, the slopes as the birthplace of catastrophes, the climate as a burden, the forests as potential farmland. When one lives with the mountains instead of merely visiting them, one accepts different values. And so it is that through the eyes of the local inhabitants I learned to see the Himalayas in a new light.

To many of the mountain people, the idea of climbing these peaks seems nearly as sacrilegious as for a devout Catholic to scale St. Peter's. Every prominent peak in the Himalayas is said to be the resort of gods or demons and is credited with supernatural powers of defence. The sacred mountain of Kangchenjunga, which means "the five jewels of eternal snow", is the place where the Tibetan god of wealth kept his treasure, and the British expedition of 1955 turned back five feet from the summit in order not to offend their Sherpas. Of Ama Dablam, Machhapuchhare, Nanda Devi and Nanga Parbat, equivalent legends are repeated at length.

The local inhabitants of the Himalayas look upon their mountains not so much with admiration as with fear or, at least, fatalism. I was walking with one of them on the slopes of Nanga Parbat through a scene of dazzling beauty, and he turned to me without any preface to remark: "The first night of marriage is the last night of love." Hoping to avoid a melancholy autobiography, I began to rhapsodize about the mountains around us. It was no good. "We who live in nature," he replied, for he had a habit of speaking in proverbs, "have no eyes with which to see it."

It is true and inevitable. The world is a cruel place, and life a constant struggle, in the plains as in the mountains. But in the mountains it is more cruel, because there all the forces of nature are ranged against men's puny efforts. They fight back, but the mountain is stronger. My companion grew bitter, recalling the friends he had lost, the labour of years destroyed overnight.

"Why do you come here?" he asked. "Do you not have kinder places in your own country?" He pointed downwards at his village. "See there, that black mark. That was our bazaar, until two weeks ago. It was burnt to the ground, not because some woman was careless with her lamp, but it was struck by lightning. And look there," swinging round to an amphitheatre of once neatly terraced slopes, now a chaos of tumbled stones. "That happened last winter, when a stream suddenly altered its course. How do you expect us to love this place?"

"Why not leave it for the plains?"

"And where in the plains? They are either desert, or already crowded with people to the point of suffocation. Let us change places: I will go to England; you can live here.'"

The catastrophes that he pointed out to me had not rated a mention even in Pakistani newspapers. They were known only to the villagers. But others on a larger scale have become history. In 1840 an ice-causeway formed on the Shyok River, creating a temporary lake 12 miles long and 400 feet deep. When it collapsed six months later, the wave was 30 feet high and did not exhaust itself until it had thundered 200 miles below. There was the winter when the Yengutsa Glacier inexplicably advanced three miles in eight days, as unstoppable as volcanic lava, to overwhelm three Hunza villages. Lower down the same valley I saw evidence of what had happened only two summers before. The river, swollen suddenly by an immense avalanche 50 miles upstream, had shorn away the cliff on which a village stood, carrying with it half the houses. The other half still stood on the verge, ruined and abandoned except for the two or three farthest from the edge which the owners had re-occupied at their peril, to be within reach of the surviving fields. Everywhere you see signs of even greater disasters, now long past but at the time creating unimaginable terror: landslides that have obliterated entire plains; rivers that have changed their courses by as much as 30 miles; earthquakes and floods that have left their mark in broken strata or streaks of a deeper colour on canyon walls. I have only to raise my eyes from where I write this, in the Hindu Kush of Afghanistan, to see on the opposite hillside a boulder as large as an omnibus, poised on a cliff-edge. It may have rested there a million years, but who can tell when it will come crashing down on the village beneath?

Thus those who live close to this wilderness view it apprehensively. It is not only impending catastrophe that menaces them, but the predictable fluctuation of climate against which they have never been able to equip themselves. There is no more pathetic sight than a Kashmiri or a Pathan shivering in the winter's cold, unless it be the same man working himself to exhaustion in the summer's heat. They have no change of clothing. The same cotton gown does duty for all seasons, and the only difference is that in winter they will take a loose fold and swathe it round their heads. A woman, too, has but one garment: she wears it every day, works in it, sleeps in it, and as likely as not it will form her shroud. It is a light sari, retaining its elegance even in extreme shabbiness, but utterly impracticable for tending flocks or cutting wood, and in cold weather lamentably inadequate.

In their dwellings one sees another aspect of the Himalayas. Built of the stone or mud or bamboo that surrounds them, many types of hut or cottage speckle the hillsides. They look pretty, but are pitiful defences against rain and cold. Leaky and draughty, lacking glass even when they have windows, damp and vermin ridden, they are traps for every infectious and pulmonary disease. In winter whole families crouch round their fire, looking up wraithlike at the passerby, sustained perhaps by a single meal a day. And what have they to look forward to? A summer of torrid heat alternating with unrelenting rain, hailstones so big that in Nepal they can incapacitate a man for weeks, and wind in gusts up to 100 miles an hour against which he can barely stand. With the humid heat come mildew and insects, recurrent spoliators of his few possessions. It is worse than a nomad's life, for the nomad can at least escape the mud and refuse of his own making.

Because of such hardships the people have been formed by the land— a hardy race inured to their wearisome life. In this world there are no roads, and man himself must often act as pack-animal. The British explorer and ornithologist Guy Mountfort quotes Hsun Tsang, a Chinese traveller who passed through these regions in A.D. 631: "Perilous were the roads and dark the gorges . . . Here were ledges hanging in mid-air; there flying bridges across abysses; elsewhere paths cut with a chisel, or footings to climb by." It is little different today. I have in my mind three pictures. One is of girls carrying on their backs large sheets of plywood that caught the wind like sails. At least this amenity of civilization might help to provide a more durable shelter. But meanwhile the journey of these girls was a purgatory, lasting many days. The second sight is of a young man with a sick friend mounted on his back, taking him—but where? There was no doctor within 50 miles. The third is of a girl, having stumbled from a footbridge with her heavy pack, struggling in the torrent below, from which she was rescued with great difficulty. Such sights are common in Nepal. Few people can afford animals to carry themselves or their burdens. We saw no mules, and the only donkeys were slung with stores for the army in the far north, a jolly cavalcade that we christened the 4th Annapurna Hussars. Even in the Kumaon Himalayas of India, where roads are plentiful, women carry on their heads loads of fodder as tall as themselves, swinging along with unself-conscious grace. The cart is unknown in the remoter regions, even where level ground pleads for its use. Within a few miles of Kathmandu, a wheelbarrow, like the

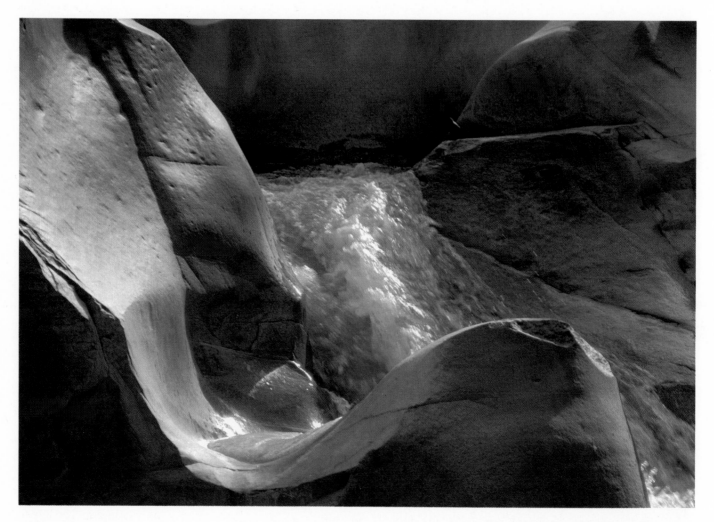

More than 10,000 feet above sea level,
one of the headstreams of the river
Ganges tumbles down its course,
through rocks carved and polished by
ice (above) and water (right). To the
Hindu faith, this part of the river is
especially sacred. Here, near its source,
below Gangotri Peak, in the Indian
Himalayas, the fast-flowing waters of the
mountain stream look very different
from the huge, sluggish river that finally
empties its muddy waters into the
Bay of Bengal, 1,500 miles away.

plough, is never seen; and this among the descendants of a people who were some of the greatest artificers and traders of the East.

Born to a life of porterage, they take it for granted, carrying burdens that would buckle the knees of most other men. I tried to lift one of the packs that our Sherpas carried to 10,000 feet. It weighed a mere 80 pounds, and nearly swung me off my feet, but to them it was no hardship or indignity. Indeed, they are quite capable of carrying loads equalling their own weight—from 150 to 180 pounds. They have developed a padding stride, unvaried for hours on end, over clusters of small loose stones, bare mountainside or steps constructed up the steeper gradients for 1,000 feet or more, like the approaches to Heaven seen in a dream. At intervals the Nepalese have built resting places, a bench to sit upon and behind it a stone table to rest the pack, and often in the centre of the table they plant a cherry or walnut tree, to give shade. You find them in places known from experience to be points of maximum exhaustion, at the top of long ascents where the ground becomes reasonably level. But for great stretches between them the path is relentless. Sometimes in traversing the length of a canyon the route is cut out of the sheer rock-face—half a tunnel, the outer side open to a precipice, and the inner hollowed to allow the passage of a crouching man. Or if the rock is too hard even for this, the path is a plank held against the canyon wall by forked trunks resting on the riverbed below.

The track is a highway, the village street its market-place. We passed beggars, merry youths, the halt and blind, a store-keeper carrying stock for a month on his back, a whole family leaving the higher ground to winter in the valley, a lama, an official of consequence in fine clothes and attended by his servant. The effect is curiously mediaeval. Because the pace is of a walk and all traffic is canalized along a single route, there is every excuse to stop and gossip: the path is a channel of communication in more than one sense. You pass and you re-pass, right and left. One has to watch the track continuously, for each stone is a dangerous new shape set at a new angle. The rhythm of ascent is different from the rhythm of descent, and there are those who say—though I am not one of them—that it is easier to go up than down. But exhaustion lies mostly in the mind: when the sun begins to shine between the boles of trees instead of through their crowns, you know you are reaching the top of the pass, and energy can flow back as rapidly as lethargy seeps in.

Then the bridges. The simplest of them are pines felled across a stream, which you must cross with a panther's tread. Others are crazily cantilevered—a design so traditional that I saw it repeated from Nepal

A Nepalese villager, accustomed since childhood to bearing heavy loads, brings a large bundle of wood up from the village. Around many high-lying villages, the trees have long since been used for firewood; those who are too poor to possess a pony or yak must collect wood themselves and carry it up the mountain to their homes.

to Afghanistan; tree trunks anchored in stone bastions on opposite banks, reaching towards each other at a slight angle till they form a gap narrow enough to be spanned by planks. But the most exciting and enjoyable are the bridges suspended from ropes of wire or twisted vines, swaying over a river a hundred feet below. They move in rhythm to every footfall—jellified cat-walks, and in places where the planks have fallen or rotted, you walk upon the wires themselves. It is not quite so dangerous as it looks, because the wires are firmly anchored and form handrails on each side. They are at their most alarming where they have been widened in the Karakorams to take Jeeps. I crossed one near Gilgit which we approached on level ground, but the far side ended at a sheer cliff-face, with a tunnel that twisted ingeniously up through the rock to gain the flat shelf above. Another bridge hung over the Astor Gorge swinging freely between its bastions.

The leeches that infest the track during the summer deserve to be pilloried in a separate paragraph of their own. They arrive with the monsoon and hang as obscenely as slugs from every bush and clump of grass, reaching out to attach themselves to passing men and animals. They penetrate to the flesh through openings as tiny as lace-holes or between the threads of woollen socks to pierce a blood-vessel with their tripartite suckers, emitting a chemical fluid that prevents the coagulation of the blood. Dozens can feed off a single limb, and so painless is their suction that a man can sleep through it, waking to find his bed-clothes soaked in blood. The wound will continue to bleed long after the leech has sucked its fill and fallen off its victim. Men are slightly better off than sheep or cows which cannot reach parts of their bodies, but it is better not to pull off a leech; this may lacerate the flesh, and the wound can turn septic. The best way to shake off a leech is with a liberal sprinkling of salt or a burning cigarette-end.

The people are a part of the mountains. Just as the mountains are majestic and unyielding, the people lead heroic lives of ceaseless toil and danger. In the most distant regions they have no outside aid. They are self-supporting, self-reliant—and nearly as unchanging as the mountains themselves. There may be a primitive open-air school for the children, but their parents behave the same, look the same and lead the same lives as their remote ancestors. The ladder by which I climbed to the flat roof of a house was hewn from a tree trunk, in much the same way as a river-canoe. Despite their sophistication in other ways, the Sherpas continue to till their fields with the *kodali*, a short-handled mattock or hoe, which has scarcely changed its form since the Stone-Age. Their medical facilities, too, are archaic. Average life expectation in Nepal is only 30 years. Goitres are commonplace and the inhabitants have never become immune to the tropical diseases, dysentery, cholera, typhoid, smallpox, jaundice and malaria. Many a devout peasant-woman will never see a doctor all her life, for shame of allowing a stranger to touch her body. In Nepal a woman came to us with her index finger half severed by an axe. Terry Spencer, who has a little more medical knowledge than I have, muttered to me that he should take the axe and complete the amputation, for the finger would probably turn gangrenous, but we disinfected and bound it, and she went away grateful for even this degree of skill in a place nine days' walk from the nearest doctor.

Fortified by inoculation against every known virus, clothed in anoraks and fur-lined boots, equipped with field-glasses, cameras and a travelling *batterie de cuisine*, we were passengers through a rocky prison in which those around us were serving lifelong sentences. We wondered whether we were wrong to pity them. If they had a road, who could afford a motor vehicle to travel it, or the luxury goods it would bring from the plains? Would tourists enrich their culture, or would they destroy it? We wished for these people the impossible: the benefits of modern technology without its penalties.

All our values were turned upside down: despite the suffering, there was cheerfulness on every side. It seemed to be proof of an astonishing resilience. And many of the villages have their simple amenities—and even a few beauties like the poinsettia, which the Nepalese plant with such abandon round their houses. An old man sitting cross-legged on a rock splitting bamboo and shaping it into baskets; a group of naked young children playing in a river; a woman slowly turning a prayer wheel—these people would not understand our compassion, nor like it if they could. All around were terraces of young maize or irrigated rice, representing the successful effort of generations; and humble beasts shared their lives and homes quasi-biblically. If the old look older and the young more vulnerable than they do in the West, none of them miss what they do not know about. Their simplicity and religion give them a peace of mind that we might envy.

I sat in a tiny mill-house in the Karakorams, frying eggs on an open fire, and talking to the group of villagers that soon collected. The background noises were the awkward churning of the mill stone, the rush of water that drove it, the spitting of the eggs. The headman of the village

A leech clings to a leaf with its powerful posterior sucker and cranes forward towards a possible host. The leech, related to the earthworm, operates like a predatory blood bank. After dropping on to a passing man or animal, it punctures the skin with its jaws and siphons off a sufficient quantity of blood to sustain it for months.

had been a sergeant in a British-Indian regiment and looked the part, but as I questioned him I felt like one of the inquisitors of a 19th-Century Highland commission:

"How high does the river rise in summer?"

"About 20 feet above what you see now."

"Does it flood the fields?"

"Sometimes; and then our crops are destroyed."

"How much rain do you have?"

"Almost none: the river is fed by melting snow."

"How do you water your crops?"

"We lead the stream-water into the fields."

"What crops do you grow?"

"Maize, buck-wheat, potatoes, rice, and some fruit, like apricots."

"What animals do you keep?"

"Goats, sheep, cows, chickens."

"Are there any wild animals or game-birds in the mountains?"

"Yes; ibex, markhor, chukkor—and once I saw a snow-leopard."

"Do you have any tools, like saws?"

"Only axes. What need have we of saws? The pine . . . ", and he glanced almost with affection at the simple roof of lashed logs, ". . . has a perfect shape for building houses. We have no need to cut it up."

"What do you obtain from outside the village?"

"We need nothing. But I have this flask that my father bought in China." (It was the largest, gaudiest tin I have ever seen.)

"How do you make clothes?"

"From sheep's wool mixed with goat-hair. We spin and weave it."

"Is the population of the village increasing?"

"It has doubled in the last 20 years."

"Do you ever go into the mountains?"

"Only to collect wood."

In his last two answers lie the most serious threats to his village, to hundreds more like it—and to the Himalayan ecology: over-population of the habitable areas and the slow destruction of the forests in the quest for cultivable land. In the 19th Century the process was called "the conquest of the forest", as if the forest were the enemy of man. It took some time to recognize it as man's greatest friend. After all, there were many peasants, and an unlimited jungle. It seemed sensible for one to clear the other. In 1848 the great naturalist and traveller Joseph Dalton Hooker watched with delight the forests of the Sikkim Himalayas going up in smoke: "At this season (April) the firing of the jungle is a frequent practice, and the effect by night is exceedingly fine: a forest so dry and full of bamboo, extending over such steep hills, afforded grand blazing spectacles. The voices of birds and insects being hushed, nothing is audible but the harsh roar of the rivers, and occasionally, rising far above it, that of the forest fires."

It is as if a man, watching a neighbour's house burn down, were to remark: "The spare bedroom is *nicely* alight now." But Hooker compounded his ignorance of what he was witnessing by adding without censure that the native of the region "never inhabits one spot for more than three successive years. He squats in any place which he can render profitable for that period, and then moves to another."

It was easier to move on after three years and burn another piece of forest because the ash does not remain a natural fertilizer for much longer. Therefore in one man's working life he might clear an area equivalent to 16 separate farms.

The effect can be seen almost anywhere in the Himalayas. The plains and lower hills are almost bare of vegetation of any kind, and the goats are busy eating what is left. It is not simply that the trees that were once there cannot grow again; the soil itself is washed away. When the rains come, both rain and earth are lost. In a forest the canopy of leaves absorbs the shock of the monsoon, so that the water reaches the ground with comparative gentleness. The trees act like sponges for the rain, retaining its moisture in the tissues of the wood and soil by a close network of roots and deep mattresses of humus, where it is protected from evaporation. The insects find a haven there, making it porous and absorbent, and every winter adds a new quota of fallen leaves and dead branches. It is a natural cycle. Now, with the trees gone, the insects die, and the water quickly runs off, carving new erosion channels and creating bare rock above and floods and landslides below. Great ravines are rapidly gouged out and large areas of plain overwhelmed by sandy outwash. The consequence is a man-made wilderness in the very places where men count most upon fertility.

Of course, there are compensations. Snow and glaciers release their waters as gradually as forests: and for generations the farmers have practised the greatest of all their skills, the terracing and irrigation of the lower slopes, which makes the most of what land and water remain. There is no more pleasing or frequent sight in the Himalayas than that of ice-cold water running swiftly in channels 40 feet above the lower plains, to drop through controlled apertures on to fields patterned like a jig-saw by their retaining walls. These considerable feats of engineering were accomplished by hand, aided by the most primitive tools. In Hunza, until quite recently, they used wooden paddles for spades, and ibex horns for picks.

In the Himalayas of northern Assam erosion is less of a problem, for the population is thin and the rain-forests immense. Few people have dared to go there, since the natives are reputed to be resentful of intruders, and thus geographers are still not quite certain how the Himalayas tail off in the east beyond Namcha Barwa. O. K. Spate, the great geographer of the Indian sub-continent, calls it one of the last unsolved topographical problems in the world.

One of the few explorers who went there was the anthropologist, C. F. Haimendorf. He took his wife with him, in order, he explained, to soften by her mere presence the indignation of the natives, a function that she accomplished with engaging charm and courage. In 1955 he published a delightful book called *Himalayan Barbary*, which did something to rehabilitate the reputation of the tribes. "The spontaneous hospitality with which we were received in the remotest villages," he wrote, "always filled me with warmth and renewed my belief in the fundamental friendliness of man." That is, so long as man is not provoked. When he is, this sort of thing can happen: "If he were to find that his wife had been unfaithful, a Dafla man would be so upset that he would be unable either to eat or sleep. He would not hesitate to kill her lover, tear him limb from limb, and show her the dismembered parts: then, roasting the flesh, he would stuff it into her mouth."

Haimendorf never reached the highest mountains that divide Assam from China, although he saw them from a distance. Once again his belief in human nature survived all his tribulations. "Far from being the treacherous savages of popular belief, the Miris of these hills struck me as cheerful companions, and the most warm-hearted of friends." On that optimistic note we can leave man in one of the two most extreme wildernesses that the Himalayas contains. The other is far fiercer: the part that lies more than 20,000 feet above the level of the sea.

Journey Through Five Realms

PHOTOGRAPHS BY CAPTAIN JOHN NOEL

The famous British expedition that attempted to conquer Everest in 1924 failed when two climbers, George Mallory and Andrew Irvine, died in an attempt on the summit. Among the survivors was photographer Captain John Noel (right). A keen amateur naturalist and a walker rather than a skilled mountaineer, Noel had been a member of a pioneering expedition to Everest two years before.

According to a contemporary account, Noel wanted "to catch and express the spirit of the mountains, the awe they inspire, their terrible character, their might and their glory, and withal their irresistible attraction". This he set out to do with a telescopic camera especially designed to work in temperatures as low as −25°F.: the mechanism to advance the film ran on ball-bearings instead of oil, which would have frozen. Noel made careful colour notes of his photographic subjects and used them later as a guide to transform his delicate black and white glass slides into hand-tinted images.

Noel's pictures provide a unique photographic record not only of the progress of the expedition, but also —as the pictures on the following pages show—of the effects of changing altitude on Himalayan vegetation. These scenes have an additional historic interest: the Nepalese government at the time forbade an approach to Everest through their territory to the south of the mountain, and so the expedition marched through Sikkim to attack Everest from Tibet—a route that has been closed to Westerners since China invaded this territory in 1950.

The expedition, which set off in March, took 35 days to reach the Base Camp, 12,000 feet below the summit. The climbers passed through five main zones of vegetation. The first hard trek through tropical jungle took them upwards to more temperate forested areas. Then they emerged to cross clear alpine pastures speckled with spring flowers, continued upwards to the almost barren Tibetan plateau, and finally reached the wasteland of ice and snow around Everest.

One of the first natural wonderlands the party traversed was the valley of the river Tista in Sikkim (far right), only 750 feet above sea level. The photograph, looking down to the river 6,000 feet below, shows the densely forested slopes that covered their route northwards.

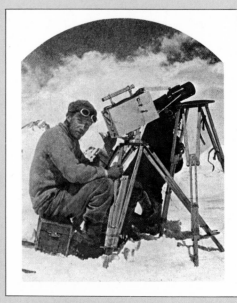

CAPTAIN NOEL AND CAMERA

THE WINDING TISTA VALLEY

CAMP IN THE FOOTHILLS

From Thick Jungle to Alpine Meadow

For the first few days, the expedition sweated through the tangled jungle of the Tista valley, where a constant 90°F. heat evaporates the drenching rains—250 inches a year—into steaming mists. Exotic butterflies and tropical birds fluttered among 20-foot high giant ferns, bamboo trees and palms entwined with creepers, vines and many varieties of orchids. The camp scene near the Tista River (left), taken by a native porter, shows Noel himself standing beside his tent, a tripod camera set for action.

At about 7,000 feet above sea level the thick jungle gradually opened out to a more temperate zone (right) where spruce, pine and other conifers grew beside oaks and magnolia trees. These upland forests were splashed with blue irises and crimson, yellow and pink rhododendrons. But as Noel and his companions reached 10,000 feet, the birch and pine trees gave way to cool green alpine pastures, carpeted with dark purple and yellow primulas, blue gentian, saxifrage and edelweiss.

UPLAND FORESTS AND MEADOWS

LAKE ON THE TIBETAN PLATEAU

Across Tibet's Stark and Lofty Plateau

As the expedition left the green alpine belt behind and below, the vegetation became scantier and the scenery increasingly desolate. This was the beginning of another world, a lofty, arid wilderness: the Tibetan Plateau. The plateau lies at an average height of 15,000 feet, extends 1,500 miles east to west and is 1,000 miles wide from north to south.

The landscape is forbidding; snow-dusted hills rise to several thousand feet above the surface of the near-barren plateau. Rainfall is minimal, but in spring rivers of melted snow and ice flow down from the mountains, supplying water to hundreds of lakes that reflect the brilliant azure sky.

Surprisingly, domestic yak herds and wild animals thrive on the area's sparse scrub. Colonel Norton (the expedition leader) observed of one occasion: "The plain appears utterly devoid of vegetation, yet herds of kyang (wild asses) and Tibetan gazelle surrounded us . . . all looking as sleek and round as if their chosen habitat were the finest pasture in Asia."

But to the climbers, the climate was as hostile as the land. Freezing nights, followed by days of bitter, piercing wind, sapped the strength of the party. "It used to be a saying among us," wrote Noel later, "that Everest's 'long arm' [the local name for the wind that batters the mountain] started to hit us before we ever reached her."

MELTWATER FROM THE RONGBUK GLACIER

At the Portals of an Ice Kingdom

A month after their departure from Darjeeling, the expedition set up Base Camp near the 50-foot thick snout of the Rongbuk Glacier, at an altitude of 16,400 feet (left).

In this realm of rock and ice dominated by the Everest massif, the wind, water and ice eat into boulder surfaces until they resemble coral. Vegetation, though restricted to meagre patches of lichen, is still enough to support some species of birds, spiders and insects, many of which are especially adapted to survive the harsh conditions of such a lofty habitat.

Higher up, at 18,000 feet on the glacier proper, the expedition encountered a fairytale world of ice pinnacles rearing up 100 feet. In Noel's photograph (right) a solitary Sherpa, on the ledge bottom to the left, is dwarfed by Rongbuk's colossal glacial spires sculptured and notched by evaporation and the driving force of the wind.

PINNACLES OF GLACIAL ICE

Towards the Great Untrodden Summit

The heights at which the climbers established the final camps on the route up Everest presented them with sublime views; but such heights also imposed treacherous and debilitating conditions. The weather, of a severity unknown in the previous 30 years, forced the climbers to turn back from several attempts on the summit. The thin air made every tiny effort a trial of willpower and physical strength.

To their surprise, they found that they were not the only living creatures to defy such altitude. Major R. Hingston, the expedition's naturalist, found tiny attid spiders in rock crevices at 22,000 feet; and choughs flew around the climbers to their highest bivouac at 27,000 feet, becoming tame and welcome companions in the wilderness.

Captain Noel, who climbed up to 23,000 feet to photograph the final assault from as close as possible, wrote of Everest: "It made a prodigious sight as I looked—a forbidding pyramid of grey and white with rugged sides. In the marvellously thin and clear air it stood bleak and menacing."

From snowfields above the Rongbuk Glacier he photographed the north-east ridge of Everest (right), dramatically lit by the evening sun. A few days later, the mountain claimed the lives of Mallory and Irvine, last seen within 600 feet of the summit, and the 1924 expedition conceded a tragic defeat.

EVENING LIGHT ON MOUNT EVEREST

7/ Into the Zone of Death

As he looks at the mountains the climber's heart swells with joy and pain. It is so beautiful and yet so inaccessible. Oh! to set foot on those virgin slopes—even though death waits poised above! EDMUND HILLARY/ *HIMALAYAS*

The peaks of the Himalayas are a different universe from the one we inhabit. One can fly over the high wilderness of snow and ice or focus on it with binoculars from the safety of the slopes thousands of feet below. But it remains remote from both the traveller and the native. Only one group of people have penetrated it—the mountaineers and their porters—and it is through their eyes that this strange universe stands revealed.

Those who challenge this wilderness are confronted by difficulties and dangers appalling in their frequency and magnitude. In the Alps, unless a climber chooses deliberately the most difficult approach, an ascent is usually predictable and well-tried. But in the Himalayas, every hazard of the lower ranges is magnified. The glaciers may be convenient routes to the summit, but they are also traps that can close with terrifying violence, breaking away in ice-blocks weighing hundreds of tons. An ice-wall a thousand feet wide and a hundred high, apparently clamped to the rock's surface, topples slowly forward in cataclysmic ruin. An avalanche of snow, fallen overnight and loosened again by the morning sun, strikes at a man with the force of a torrent and carries him helpless over a precipice. If he tries to avoid these dangers by ascending the ridges, a whole new category of risks awaits him. The knife-edge is so sharp, its sides so steep, that a single moment of inattention can plunge him to his death. An ice-cornice suddenly collapses under his added weight. A slab of rock sloping like a roof-tile, one of a thousand others safely traversed, is found, too late, to be unsupported.

The weather is equally unpredictable. Sometimes the sun can be so violent, piercing the thin air with X-ray intensity doubled by reflection from the snow, that a man can suffer as acutely from sunburn as in an equatorial desert; that same night he may endure agonies of polar cold. The range of temperature at these altitudes is extraordinary: it has been measured as high as 119° F. in direct sunlight, and as low as —40° F. at night. The wind can suddenly rise to hurricane force, filling the air with snow to create an airborne avalanche against which a climber cannot stand. His tent, if he has one, can be as difficult to erect as to furl a mainsail in a gale, or it may be whipped from his sleeping body. Such gales can last for weeks, making all movement, upwards or downwards, impossible. At the start of their successful attempt on K2 in 1954 the Italians were scarcely able to move from their tents for 40 days. In 1934 Willy Merkl, the German climber, was isolated by a blizzard on Nanga Parbat and endured nine torturing days of cold and starvation until he died in a snowdrift, where his body was found four years later.

Then there is the debilitating effect of altitude. Acclimatization helps, but nobody can predict its effect. A young man, perhaps the strongest in a team, like Mario Puchoz on K2, can die suddenly of pneumonia. Another will be attacked by phlebitis. Age seems to have little to do with it. Mountaineers are not Olympic athletes. The age fittest for the mountains seems to lie between 25 and 40, since experience has shown that younger men do not have the physical or mental stamina.

Altitude can totally alter a man's character. The will is weakened; friendship is threatened. "Your friend in civilization," Frank Smythe, the conqueror of Kamet, has written, "may become your enemy on a mountain; his very snore assumes a new and repellent note; his tricks at the mess-table, the sound of his mastication, the scarcely concealed triumph with which he appropriates the choicest tit-bits, the absurd manner in which he walks, even the cut of his clothes and the colour of the patch on the seat of his trousers, may induce an irritation and loathing almost beyond endurance."

The ascent of Annapurna I by Maurice Herzog and his party of Frenchmen in 1950 provides what is perhaps the most dramatic example of the Himalayas' effect on man; it also produced one of mountaineering's finest books, *Annapurna*, Herzog's own account of the expedition's achievements and ordeals. No mountain over 26,000 feet had ever been climbed before. Nepal was opened to Westerners only that year.

The country was quite unknown, the approaches to Annapurna unexplored, and the local porters unorganized and untrained. Judging by the experience of climbers in British India during the previous half-century, it seemed impossible that so formidable a peak could be reconnoitred and climbed at the first attempt. But this is what the Frenchmen achieved, and their story still arouses wonder and vicarious suffering.

They had originally intended to climb Dhaulagiri (26,810 feet), but were beaten by its crevasses and a 15,000-foot wall, twice as high as the north face of the Eiger, and switched their effort across the Kali Gandaki Valley to Annapurna I, 26,504 feet high. The early stages of the ascent were very difficult, but Herzog himself (unusual for an expedition's leader) and one companion, Louis Lachenal, were in good condition when they found themselves at the highest camp poised for the summit attempt. In Herzog's words, "We took it in turns to make the track, and often stopped without any word having passed between us. Each of us lived in a closed and private world of his own . . . We remembered the days of marching in sweltering heat, the hard pitches we had overcome, the tremendous efforts we had all made to lay siege to the mountain, the daily heroism of all my friends in establishing the camps. Now we were nearing our goal. In an hour or two perhaps victory would be ours. Must we give up? No, that would be impossible. My whole being revolted against the idea. Today we were consecrating an ideal, and no sacrifice was too great. An astonishing happiness welled up in me." It was not to last for long.

They reached the summit at 3 p.m. on June 3, 1950, photographed each other, and pulled from the bottom of their rucksack a French pennant, stained with sweat and stale food. Then their troubles began. As they started down, one of Herzog's gloves blew away. He realized what this meant—"the start of a race with death". Lachenal stumbled ahead, sensing that his feet were freezing. At the highest camp they found two of their friends, Lionel Terray and Gaston Rébuffat, to whom they told the news of their success, but when Terray clasped Herzog's hand in congratulation, he found it as hard and cold as stone, white and violet with frostbite. Lachenal had lost ice-axe, cap, gloves and one crampon in a fall, his feet and both hands were frozen solid, and he was in a state of semi-delirium. All that night the fresher men worked on their two friends, massaging their numbed limbs. In the morning a gale-force blizzard was blowing. The four of them set out again with only two ice-axes between them, and the mist and snow were so thick that they could scarcely see from one end of the rope to the other.

Snow whirls above Lhotse whipped by winds that, funneling through a valley below the mountain, are forced up by the immense wall of rock.

Sinking up to their waists in new snow, they searched vainly for the camp below, where they knew help awaited them. Failing to find it, they spent the night in a vertical tunnel of ice, huddling together to share the warmth of their bodies, talking in signs more than words. "There was still a breath of life in me," wrote Herzog, "but it dwindled steadily as the hours went by. Was this cavern not the most beautiful grave I could hope for?" In the early morning an avalanche spread into it, half burying them. Terray and Rébuffat struggled out, only to find that the previous day's exertions had left them snow-blind. So they were now four men, two crippled, two blind, all lost. Herzog whispered to Terray, "Lionel, I am dying." They shouted for help: their voices carried only ten feet in the gale. Somehow they struggled on, the maimed now leading the blind. With inexpressible relief they discovered that the camp was only 200 yards from the hole where they had spent the night, and two Frenchmen and four Sherpas were there to help them. The farther journey was slow torture, but the will to live had returned. They descended ice-walls by rope, but frostbite made their efforts so clumsy that the skin was torn from their hands and hung in strips. They reached Camp II, still at 20,000 feet, and there was the expedition's doctor, who injected their arteries with azetylcholin to stimulate the agonizing recirculation of the blood.

That was not the end of their ordeal. Camp II was turned into a casualty clearing station, but it was no hospital. The men must be taken down at once to save their lives. Herzog and Lachenal were gently lowered from ledge to ledge until they reached the valley, and from that point they were carried on stretchers for three weeks in the pouring rain of the monsoon to the Indian frontier. The doctor snipped off their fingers and toes one by one to prevent the spread of gangrene to their whole bodies. All Lachenal's toes were amputated: Herzog lost all his toes and all his fingers.

Why then do they do it? Many of the world's greatest climbers find it difficult to explain. At Kathmandu I met one of the American mountaineers who reached the summit of Everest in 1963. He was a short man, built like a jockey, who bore on his young face the marks of great exertion; the skin around his eyes was lined like a sailor's. He and three companions had survived a night at 28,000 feet without tent or sleeping-bags, but fortunately there had been no wind. I asked him whether it was true that a sort of euphoria numbs the senses when one is in this lofty wilderness. "Well," he replied, "only in so far as you feel quite isolated from your companions. You are in a world of your own. If

A monstrous avalanche—released by
warm weather, rain or sudden vibration
—hurtles down the 25,850-foot Nuptse
ridge, near Mount Everest (left). In its
fearsome descent it dislodges thousands
of tons of piled snow and flings them
billowing down the valley.

you have to talk, you do so by signals or grunts. You cannot speak and breathe simultaneously at that height. I felt at one moment that I wouldn't live through it. Then suddenly, at about 4 a.m., came the realization that I would survive. That was the best moment: you might say that it was the only happy moment. When I got to the top, I had thought only of the enormous difficulty of getting down. It was like being in combat. Only a day or two later, when the lower camps had nursed us down, did I experience any sense of achievement and triumph. I looked back at Everest and thought, 'Was I really there? Well, I need never go there again.' " And then he added, as so many other climbers do: "I can't think why it is that I go on doing it."

It cannot be because they enjoy the mountain scenery. Danger and exhaustion and sickness of mind and body dull the appreciation of natural beauty, and rarely can a climber lift his eyes from the place where his next footstep will fall. If they loved mountains for their splendour, they would walk the foothills parallel to the crest, as I did. Mountaineers are only interested in height and the Himalayas offer the greatest heights of all. Achievement is measured in hundreds and thousands of feet, vertically, and for them the mountain has no other dimension. Sometimes, however, a climber of unusual sensibility, like Christian Bonington, will pause to contemplate with wonder the devastation around him. For devastation it is. There is no construction here, except very temporarily; only destruction, and it can take ugly as well as terrifying forms. A glacier that has lost its snow is "a mournful place of grit-covered ice, decaying towers and dark, yawning holes", as Bonington wrote of the glacier that sweeps up to the south face of Annapurna. "In bright sunlight it is like an abandoned scrapyard." Only the mist and the moon can soften hard outlines, obliterate the hideous detail of decay and flood gloomy sockets with translucency.

It is the view from the mountains, not the view the struggling climber has of his own painful route, that fills with occasional rapture a mind however tired. The neighbouring summits seem beautiful: the summit immediately above rarely does. But it is the view downwards that exalts the spirit—the ice giving place to rock, the rock to scrub, the scrub to trees, the distant trees to cultivation and the unseen life of the valleys and the plains. It is the view, as in an historical diorama, of the emergence of man.

A wilderness presumes a non-wilderness, and when both are visible simultaneously, the effect of both is magnified. You can see them in juxtaposition, comfortably from below; but how much more eloquent is the contrast from above! There are no seasons here. You are isolated in a prehistoric world, a frozen world, where even a bee's sting would be a welcome reminder of things known. But there are no bees. Nature is shorn of its gentle impertinences and of all its delicacy except for the changing colours. You are confronted by the rawest elements of which the globe is made. It is a miserable world, yet sublime.

All this comes to the mountaineer, however, only in retrospect. During the climb, far from being an object of admiration, the mountain is an enemy. "The five of us sat that night in an atmosphere of hatred for the mountains," said Ian Rowe of the unsuccessful attempt on Dhaulagiri in 1973. "All we now wanted was to get off." Mountaineers conceive their adventures in para-military terms. The very language of mountaineering reveals it: expedition, assault, conquest, defeat. Their camps, like army corps, are identified with Roman numerals from I to VIII or IX. Just as a soldier can respect his enemy, so the mountaineer is humbled by his failure. "We slugged into Kathmandu," wrote Dennis Gray after his unsuccessful attempt on the 23,400-foot Gauri Sankar, "weary, dejected, unwashed, ragged, fed up with ourselves and with each other. The mountain gleamed high in the sky on the horizon, a reminder that time would heal the wounds."

What is it that drives a man to risk his very life on the summits? Undoubtedly, there is an element of glory-seeking, personal or patriotic, as there is in war. Karl Herrligkoffer assembled his party at the base of Nanga Parbat to pledge themselves to victory in "an Olympic oath" for the honour of Germany. When the Italians reached the summit of K2, Ardito Desio, their leader, issued an order of the day: "Lift up your hearts, dear comrades. By your efforts you have won great glory for your native land." The British, the Americans, the French, the Japanese and the Russians have been equally aware that national prestige is involved in their efforts.

But the greatest attraction, of course, is the danger, which this environment presents as no other can. The mountains offer the opportunity to test nerve, skill and endurance to the limit. The mountaineers are driven by that streak in men, as Robin Lane Fox wrote of Alexander the Great, that drives them to dare what other men have not thought possible. Take away the hazards, says John Hunt, leader of the successful British expedition to Everest in 1953, and you will rob mountaineering of its pleasure. Long before anyone thought of climbing the Himalayas, Byron, who might almost have had mountaineers in mind, put it thus:

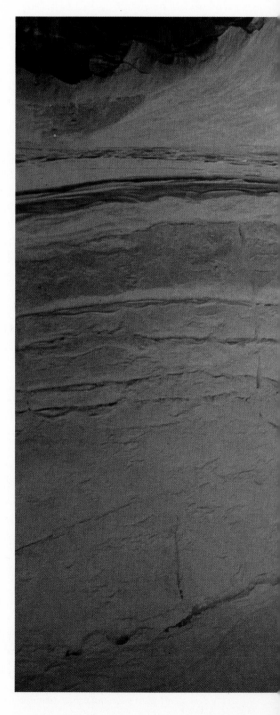

Perils he sought not, but ne'er shrank to meet;
The scene was savage, but the scene was new;
This made the ceaseless toil of travel sweet.
Beat back keen winter's blast, and welcomed summer's heat.
And Francis Younghusband: "What is the secret of it? Quite certainly it is the power of the mountains to force the best out of men. Man likes to be his best. But often nothing short of a Himalayan peak can extract it from him, can compel him to be fittest in body, alertist in mind and firmest in soul." Wilfred Noyce has written: "By climbing mountains, by extending himself beyond the bounds of everyday experience, a man can set up a new relationship with something bigger than himself."

Because mountaineering is a matter of the spirit and the emotions, the reactions of the mountaineers differ. To some, the scaling of a peak is the infinite magnification of a child's pleasure in treading a lawn of virgin snow. "The contest," said Edmund Hillary, who reached the summit of Everest in the 1953 assault, "brings fear and joy—and a deep respect, whatever the result of the struggle". The greys of ordinary life become blacks and whites. To some, the barren wastes are places where a man can be alone with himself and his God. To succeed is almost a sacrilege, like shooting a tiger. Bill Tilman wrote of his conquest of Nanda Devi in 1936: "The feeling which predominated over all was one of remorse at the fall of a giant."

Sometimes normal emotions are suspended. When Dougal Haston and Don Whillans reached the top of Annapurna by the south face, in 1970, "there was only a kind of numbness". Smythe wrote of his ascent to the Mana peak: "It was as though I had been led blindfold up the mountain, and the bandage had been removed on the summit. But of all my memories, one stands pre-eminent: the silence. The silence of dead places where not even a plant grows or a bird dwells . . . I seemed on the very boundary of things knowable and unknowable."

Others have found themselves over the boundary, into hallucination, and Smythe himself, climbing alone on Everest in 1933, was convinced that he was roped to another man. So clear was the impression that he divided his piece of cake into two. Later he saw, in a mirage, two kites hanging motionless before him in the air. On Nanga Parbat Hermann Buhl turned to talk to a friend who he knew, with another part of his mind, was not there. Herbert Tichy, who also experienced this condition, said there was nothing terrifying about it. It arises because the mind is not anchored by the bonds of reason, as it is lower down, and seems to roam freely to the very verge of insanity. Extreme

An English mountaineering team skirting the gaping jaws of a massive crevasse in the Western Cwm of Everest in 1972.

cold and lack of oxygen, added to great exhaustion, engenders a sense of complete indifference, and conjures up phantom companions.

Such is the scale of the mountains that it is difficult to imagine the success of an unsupported climber. Solo attempts on Himalayan peaks have always ended in failure. Friends, in the flesh, become a spur to success, an insurance against danger. An expedition is a team. The planning of it, from its conception in a Welsh pub or a Zürich inn—what Lord Hunt calls "the mental preparation"—the long approach march, the establishment of lower camps, the shared hazards and exhilaration, create a spirit of joint endeavour that pushes men to the limits of endurance. The process is one of slow pyramidical building, the reduction of tons of stores at the base camp to the last bottle of oxygen that will make the difference (as to Hillary in 1953) between success and failure at the top.

The total effort may be in the order of one-tenth climbing and nine-tenths porterage, forcing the flow of supplies to run uphill, and this can only be achieved by collaboration. Rivalry and envy, so far as this is humanly possible, are suppressed. The success of one is the triumph of all. Routes and camps can be planned but not settled in advance. The variety of circumstances being infinite, success depends upon such small things as the angle of a rock-face, the breadth of a cornice, the position of a hand- or toe-hold, an illness, the loss of a crampon, a change in weather—in fact, the element of chance that man cannot foretell.

It all began in the Alps in the 18th Century. Techniques of mountain-climbing were evolved; a literature was created. When the major Alpine peaks had been climbed, men looked farther afield, and higher, and the Himalayas became their natural target, for there their sights could be raised to the limit. The surveyors led the way, because the British needed more information about India's northern frontiers, and many accomplished extraordinary journeys. In 1855 Adolphe and Robert Schlagintweit, two brothers employed by the Magnetic Survey, approached Kamet from the Tibetan side and reached 22,300 feet.

The first northern circuit of Everest, from Darjeeling to Kathmandu, was made in 1871. In 1895 came the first attempt to climb a major peak as an exploit for its own sake, when A. F. Mummery, an experienced British Alpinist, was killed on Nanga Parbat. The first monster peak to fall was Trisul (23,382 feet), to Tom Longstaff in 1907. Everest was first attempted in 1922, and in 1924 came the gallant deaths of George Leigh Mallory and Andrew Irvine, which created a legend still familiar 50 years later to every schoolboy. In 1931 Kamet fell to Frank Smythe. In 1936

Bill Tilman and N. E. Odell climbed Nanda Devi. But none of the supreme mountains—the 13 that top 26,000 feet—was climbed until after the Second World War. Now all of them have been, some several times.

What, it may be wondered, is there left to do? Plenty. There are several famous peaks like Macchapuchhare (22,950 feet) that have not been climbed to the top, and others of equivalent height have hardly been explored. There are more difficult routes to attempt up mountains already climbed, like Annapurna's south face, which was conquered by Chris Bonington's expedition of 1970, and the south-west face of Everest, which he attempted in 1972. There is the challenge to smaller parties to repeat the achievements of previous expeditions that were backed by great resources of money and manpower.

No doubt, too, the technological aids to climbing will continue to evolve. The Victorians would use no gear that "modified the face of the mountain", allowing only the cutting of ice-steps, since ice (they argued illogically) was not part of the mountain. They climbed in knicker-bockers and motoring gloves. When special clothing, crampons and pitons were introduced, the old-stagers condemned those who used the new climbing aids for "throwing unwarrantable resources at magnifi-cent peaks". Oxygen was worse, and early expeditions climbed without it. Then a more realistic attitude became acceptable. On Hunt's 1953 expedition to Everest, they carried extensible aluminium ladders, rope ladders, pulleys, a light mortar to bring down avalanches, radios, special high-altitude clothing and newly designed tents. On K2 in 1954 the Italians used a ropeway to slide stores up the steepest slopes by a hand-operated windlass. Then came the use of aircraft to cut out the exhausting rigours of the long approach march.

But no artificial aids can prevent the ultimate confrontation between men and the merciless defences of nature. Nothing can mitigate the awfulness of crumpled, ice-coated rocks, the violence of an avalanche or blizzard, the terror of a slip at great heights. This book has been about a wilderness. If wilderness is what men seek as a refuge from their civilizations and as a test of their courage, here in the Himalayas above 25,000 feet, in what Herbert Tichy called his "zone of death", they will find it untamed, in perpetuity.

Celestial Heights

Mountain peaks are never really conquered. Man may stand on them boastfully—for a moment after a struggle to the top—but his victory is short-lived. To the people of the Himalayas this is as it should be, since to them the peaks constitute a wilderness apart, the rightful dwelling place not of men, but of the gods. The rolling clouds and shades of light captured in the pictures on these pages may vary, but the massiveness of these regal monoliths conveys a sense of the Eternal.

To the Hindus the Himalayas are central to their cosmology. The peaks are the petals of the Golden Lotus that the god Vishnu created as a first step in the formation of the universe. On one of these peaks, Mt. Kailas, sits Shiva in a state of perpetual meditation, generating the spiritual force that sustains the cosmos. And when Vishnu caused the Ganges to flow from Heaven, he made it reach the Earth on the highest peaks where Shiva caught it up in his eyebrow.

To the Tibetans the Himalayan peaks are the sacred ground for a multitude of gods and devils. On one peak dwells the red goddess who owns a nine-headed tortoise, on another, the brown goddess who rides a turquoise-maned horse, and on a third 361 demons, all brothers.

The names of many peaks reflect this mystical tradition. The highest of them all, Everest, is called Chomolungma by the Tibetans, meaning Goddess Mother of the Earth. Annapurna translates as Giver of Life. The mountain richest in Tibetan mythology is Kangchenjunga: Five Treasures of the Eternal Snows. Tibetans believe that the god of wealth lives there, storing on its five peaks the five treasures: gold, silver, copper, corn and sacred books.

In 1955, Kangchenjunga's divinity threatened a British climbing expedition. The governments of Sikkim, India and Nepal refused to allow the climb because their peoples feared that the enterprise might provoke the anger of the god and bring serious harm to the land. Eventually a compromise was reached. The climbers halted within a stone's throw of the summit; the Sherpas buried offerings to their god; and the group went back down the mountain without defiling the holy peak. Such deference was once articulated by a Hindu pilgrim, who said, "In the midst of such peaks, one can draw near to what is truly placeless, the really divine."

KANGTEGA IN A CORONET OF CLOUDS

THAMSERKU AT SUNRISE

KANGCHENJUNGA LOOMING IN A DISTANT HAZE

MACHHAPUCHHARE, "THE FISH'S TAIL," A SYMBOL OF VISHNU

NUPTSE, THE WESTERN OUTPOST OF EVEREST

ANNAPURNA, "GIVER OF LIFE"

EVEREST AT SUNSET

Bibliography

Bauer, Paul, *The Siege of Nanga Parbat.* Rupert Hart-Davis, 1956.

Bonington, Chris, *Annapurna South Face.* Cassell, 1971.

Bonington, Chris, *Everest, South West Face.* Hodder and Stoughton, 1973.

Calder, Nigel, *Restless Earth.* BBC Publications, 1972.

Corbett, Jim, *Man-eaters of Kumaon.* Oxford University Press, 1944.

Cornwall, Ian, *Ice Ages: Their Nature and Effects.* John Baker Ltd., 1970.

Desio, Ardito, *Ascent of K2.* Elek Books, 1955.

Dyhrenfurth, G. O., *To the Third Pole.* Werner Laurie, 1955.

Dyson, James L., *The World of Ice.* Cresset Press, 1963.

Eiselin, Max, *The Ascent of Dhaulagiri.* Oxford University Press, 1961.

Etherton, P. T., *Across the Roof of the World.* Constable and Co., 1911.

Fraser-Tytler, W. K., *Afghanistan.* Oxford University Press, 1950.

Fukada, Kyuya, *The Great Himalayas.* Abrams, 1973.

Gee, E. P., *The Wild Life of India.* Collins, 4th edition, 1969.

Gray, Dennis, *Rope Boy.* Gollancz, 1970.

Hagen, Toni, *Mount Everest.* Oxford University Press, 1963. (includes contributions by G. O. Dyhrenfurth, C. F. Haimendorf and E. Schneider).

Hagen, Toni, *Nepal.* Kunnerley and Frey, Berne, 1961.

Haimendorf, C. F., *Himalayan Barbary.* John Murray, 1955.

Herrligkoffer, Karl M., *Nanga Parbat.* Elek Books, 1954.

Herzog, Maurice, *Annapurna.* Jonathan Cape, 1952.

Heuvelmans, Bernard, *On the Track of Unknown Animals.* Paladin, 1970.

Hillary, Edmund, *High Adventure.* Hodder and Stoughton, 1955.

Hindley, Geoffrey, *The Roof of the World.* Aldus Books, 1971.

Hooker, J. D., *Himalayan Journals* (2) (2 vols.). John Murray, 1854.

Hooker, J. D. and Thomson, T., *Introductory Essay to Flora Indica.* W. Pamplin, 1855.

Hooker, J. D. and W. J. Hooker, ed., *Rhododendrons of Sikkim-Himalaya.* Reeve, 1849.

Hunt, John, *The Ascent of Everest.* Hodder and Stoughton, 1953.

Huxley, Leonard, *Life and Letters of J. D. Hooker.* John Murray, 1918.

Izzard, Ralph, *The Abominable Snowman Adventure.* Hodder and Stoughton, 1955.

Jackson, John A., *More than Mountains.* George G. Harrap and Co., 1955.

Lane Fox, Robin, *Alexander the Great.* Allan Lane, 1973.

Leifer Walter, *Himalaya: Mountains of Destiny.* Galley Press Ltd., 1962.

Long, Tony, *Mountain Animals.* Macdonald, 1971.

Maraini, Fosco, *Where Four Worlds Meet.* Hamish Hamilton Ltd., 1964.

Mason, Kenneth, *Abode of Snow.* Rupert Hart-Davis, 1955.

Mountford, Guy, *The Vanishing Jungle.* Collins, 1969.

Murray, W. H., *The Story of Everest 1921-1952.* J. M. Dent and Sons Ltd., 1953.

Nebesky-Wojkowitz, René von, *Where the Gods are Mountains.* Weidenfeld and Nicolson, 1956.

Newby, Eric, *A Short Walk in the Hindu Kush.* Hodder and Stoughton, 1958.

Noel, Captain J. B. L., *Through Tibet to Everest.* Edward Arnold and Co., 1927.

Norton, Lt-Col. E. F., *The Fight for Everest 1924.* Edward Arnold and Co., 1925.

Noyce, Wilfred, *Climbing the Fish's Tail.* William Heinemann, 1958.

Prater, S. H., *The Book of Indian Animals.* Bombay Natural Historical Society, 3rd edition, 1971.

Salim, Ali, *Indian Hill Birds.* Oxford University Press, 1949.

Sayed Khan Qamer, A., *The Lure of the Karakorams.* Rawalpindi, 1973.

Shirakawa, Yoshikazu, *Himalayas.* Tokyo, 1971. (Includes contributions by Edmund Hillary, Arnold Toynbee.)

Smythe, F. S., *Kamet Conquered.* Gollancz, 1932.

Smythe, F. S., *The Valley of Flowers.* Hodder and Stoughton, 1938.

Spate, O. H. K., *India and Pakistan,* Methuen, 1954.

Stainton, J. D. A., *Forests of Nepal.* John Murray, 1972.

Swinson, Arthur, *North West Frontier.* Hutchinson, 1967.

Tichy, Herbert, *Himalaya.* Hale, 1971.

Tilman, H. W., *The Ascent of Nanda Devi.* Cambridge University Press, 1937.

Tilman, H. W., *Nepal Himalaya.* Cambridge University Press, 1952.

Whistler, Hugh, *Popular Handbook of Indian Birds.* Gurney and Jackson, 1928.

Wood, Captain John, *Journey to the Source of the Oxus.* John Murray, 1872.

Younghusband, Sir Francis, *The Epic of Mount Everest.* Edward Arnold and Co., 1926.

Younghusband, Sir Francis, *Everest: The Challenge.* Thomas Nelson and Sons Ltd., 1936.

Younghusband, Captain Frank E., *The Heart of a Continent,* John Murray, 1896.

Acknowledgements

The author and editors of this book wish to thank the following: Jack Amos, London; Mike Cheyney, Kathmandu; Dr. C. Embleton, London; Robert E. Fleming, Kathmandu; Sally Foy, London; Dr. Colin Harrison, Tring; Imtiaz Hussein, Rawalpindi; Tony Long, Rye; Susan Pinkus, London; The Library of Royal Botanical Gardens, Kew; Captain John Noel, New Romney; The Library of Royal Geographical Society, London; G. C. Tripathi, Ranikhet.

Picture Credits

Sources for pictures in this book are shown below. Credits for pictures from top to bottom are separated by dashes.

Cover—Jim Burke, Time-Life Picture Agency, 1965, Time Incorporated. Front end papers 1, 2—Dorothy Mierow. Front end paper 3, page 1—Raghubir Singh. 2, 3—Goetz D. Plage from Bruce Coleman Ltd., London. 4, 5—F. Jackson from Robert Harding Associates, London. 6, 7—Su Gooders from Ardea Photographics, London. 8, 9—B. N. Kelly. 10, 11—S. V. Kimber. 12, 13—G. Bell. 18, 19—Maps by Hunting Surveys Ltd., London. 25—Mark Boulton. 27—N. A. Callow from Natural History Photographic Agency, Westerham, Kent. 30, 31—Eileen Tweedy, courtesy of The Director, Royal Botanic Gardens, Kew. 35—G. Bell. 36, 37—John Cleare. 38—B. N. Kelly. 39—Christopher Grey-Wilson. 40, 41—Mark Boulton. 42, 43—Christopher Grey-Wilson from Robert Harding Associates. 46, 47—B. N. Kelly. 49—Hunting Surveys Ltd. 52, 53—G. S. Bishop C.B., O.B.E. 56 to 63—Terence Spencer. 66—Gustav R. Zimek from Tierbilder Okapia, Frankfurt. 69—Wilfried D. Schurig from Tierbilder Okapia. 70—Richard Waller from Ardea Photographics. 74, 75—Eric Shipton F.R.G.S., courtesy of the Royal Geographical Society, London. 79—John Gooders from Ardea Photographics. 80—M. D. England from Ardea Photographics. 81—M. Krishnan from Ardea Photographics. 82, 83—Goetz D. Plage from Survival Anglia Ltd., London. 84, 85—Mark Boulton. 86, 87—John Gooders from Ardea Photographics. 93—George Schaller from Bruce Coleman Inc., New York. 95—Harrison Forman, New York. 101—George Silk, Time-Life Picture Agency, 1972, Time Incorporated. 102—G. J. Broekhuyson from Ardea Photographics. 103 to 105—Goetz D. Plage from Bruce Coleman Ltd. 106—Robert L. Fleming from Ardea Photographics. 107—Goetz D. Plage from Bruce Coleman Ltd. 108, 109—Robert L. Fleming from Ardea Photographics. 113—Harrison Forman. 115—Goetz D. Plage from Bruce Coleman Ltd. 119—Nancy Tapper. 120—Christopher Grey-Wilson. 122, 123—F. Jackson from Robert Harding Associates. 127—Christopher Grey-Wilson from Robert Harding Associates. 128—Goetz D. Plage from Bruce Coleman Ltd. 129 to 135—Christopher Grey-Wilson from Robert Harding Associates. 140—Raghubir Singh. 141—Jim Burke, Time-Life Picture Agency, 1965, Time Incorporated. 142—Terence Spencer. 144—Christopher Grey-Wilson from Robert Harding Associates. 148 to 157—Captain John Noel. 161—B. N. Kelly. 163—G. S. Bishop C.B., O.B.E. 167—Christian Bonington. 171—B. N. Kelly. 172, 173—Goetz D. Plage from Survival Anglia Ltd. 174—Keith Hyatt from Natural Science Photos, London. 175—Terence Spencer. 176—B. N. Kelly. 177—N. A. Callow from Natural History Photographic Agency. 178, 179—G. S. Bishop C.B., O.B.E.

Index

Numerals in italics indicate a photograph or drawing of the subject mentioned.